HOUDINI

Houdini

The Elusive American

ADAM BEGLEY

Yale

UNIVERSITY
PRESS

New Haven and London

Yale University Press books may be purchased in quantity for educational, business, or promotional use. For information, please e-mail sales.press@yale.edu (U.S. office) or sales@yaleup.co.uk (U.K. office).

Set in Janson type by Integrated Publishing Solutions.
Printed in the United States of America.

Frontispiece: Library of Congress, LC-USZC4-3277.

Library of Congress Control Number: 2019947803
ISBN 978-0-300-23079-6 (hardcover : alk. paper)

A catalogue record for this book is available from the British Library.

This paper meets the requirements of ANSI/NISO Z39.48-1992
(Permanence of Paper).

10 9 8 7 6 5 4 3 2 1

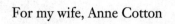

For my wife, Anne Cotton

CONTENTS

HOUDINI

The Chinese Water Torture Cell

THE GREAT HOUDINI, America's peerless self-liberator, strides onto the stage, resplendent in evening dress, flanked by three assistants, their purple uniforms adorned with gold brocade, polished brass buckets at the ready. He stands near a curious contraption, a mahogany and glass chamber about the shape and size of a telephone booth. He calls it his Chinese Water Torture Cell. In slow staccato rhythms he describes the fearsome apparatus, claiming it as his "original invention." He says, "I am willing to forfeit the sum of $1,000 to anyone who can prove that it is possible to obtain air inside the Torture Cell when I am locked up in it in the regulation manner after it has been filled with water." Solicitous of his audience, he reassures us that in case of emergency, one of his assistants will be standing by with an ax, ready to smash the half-inch-thick tempered glass, "allowing the water to flow out in order to save my life." His smile is a slice of fierce energy. The ax is already onstage, its gleaming blade biting into a wooden block. "I positively and honestly do not expect any accident to happen, but we all know accidents *will* happen—and when least expected."

After inviting a committee from the audience to examine the cell, he exits the stage to prepare himself for his ordeal, while his assistants don foul-weather gear and wellies. Once the inspection is complete, the torture cell is filled with water from the brass buckets. Houdini returns in a dressing gown. He removes it. Clad only in a blue bathing costume, he lies down on his back to have his feet clamped in heavy stocks, like a criminal submitting to cruel punishment. Offstage winches turn, and the stocks slowly rise, lifting the magician's legs, hoisting him up over the cell. When he is hanging upside down directly above it, he takes a deep breath, claps his hands, then folds his arms across his chest. He's slowly lowered into the gruesome chamber, displaced water spilling over the sides as he descends. Padlocks secure a grill at the top. Through the glass panels we can see how tightly he's jammed in; we can imagine the terror, the panicked certainty that escape is impossible.

An assistant draws a curtain around the cell, the orchestra strikes up "Asleep in the Deep"—a dirge to the drowned. Seconds tick by, all of us in the audience fear the worst . . . a minute has passed, two minutes. Surely Houdini's doom is sealed—won't an assistant swing the ax? No! Here he is, dripping wet, throwing back the curtain to reveal the torture cell, still locked, the water inside gently sloshing. Once again the Great Houdini has cheated death!

Today we know that the secret of the spectacular Water Torture Cell illusion is mechanical (the ingenious construction of the apparatus). And yet without Houdini's exceptional skill (a supreme mastery of his own fantastically strong and supple body), without courage, without showmanship, the trick would have failed—catastrophically. He relied on human qualities, insisting that there was nothing supernatural about his dazzling, baffling feats.

This book does not set out to answer the question *How did he do it?* As Houdini wisely remarked when asked: "If you knew, you would not consider the feat marvelous or even interesting." Magic explained loses its luster. The question addressed in these pages is *Why?* Why did he shackle and torture himself, even once he was rich and famous, a household name? Surely there was no longer any need to hazard his life, to dangle nine stories above a crowded avenue, suspended by the ankles and laced into a straitjacket; no need to hurl himself off a bridge into a freezing river, hands and feet manacled. Why repeat these harrowing ordeals, courting death each time? Must a self-liberator also be a self-torturer? Instead of retiring as he occasionally threatened to do, he persisted, adding new twists to his daredevil escapes even as his body aged, ramping up the risk as his hair turned gray. He carried on, stripping naked and offering his wrists to cuffs, his legs to irons, punishing himself and tempting fate until the day he died. What kind of man was this?

1

◆◆◆

A Father's Legacy

AT THE PINNACLE of his fame as an escape artist, Harry Houdini wrote a poignant account of a family disaster that struck when he was a boy, the day in 1882 when his father lost his job as a rabbi: "One morning my father awoke to find himself thrown upon the world, his long locks of hair having silvered in service, with seven children to feed, without a position, and without any visible means of support. . . . Such hardships and hunger became our lot that the less said on the subject the better."

The gist of the passage—the dire predicament of a destitute family—is more or less accurate, but the pathos is undercut by a blatant untruth in the sentence that precedes it: "My birth occurred April 6th, 1874, in the small town of Appleton, in the State of Wisconsin, U.S.A." Houdini was born in Budapest, Hungary, not Appleton, Wisconsin (and on March 24, not April 6). An immigrant like his parents and four Hungarian-born siblings, he arrived in the United States when he was four years old, deposited in New York City by the SS *Frisia*, an iron-hulled German steamship. (Two younger siblings were American-born, as he clearly wished to be.) His father, who called himself the Reverend Doctor Mayer Samuel Weiss, served as rabbi for the small Jewish community in Appleton; after four years in the post, he was indeed summarily dismissed, when Houdini (then Ehrich Weiss) was eight. Hardship and hunger ensued.

For the father, age fifty-three, this was the beginning of a dismal downward trajectory that ended with his death a decade later. After a promising start, his American life turned sour, a punishing sequence of petty humiliations. The son saw the father's failure as a trap. Avoiding that trap was at first a reflex, the earliest stirring of his impulse to escape—the impulse that transformed him into his ideal self, a world-famous unbeatable American superhero. (Another spur was America itself, the expansive opportunity his father was unable to grasp.) He liked to reassure his audiences, "I, the true Houdini, will never fail you."

The firing of the Reverend Doctor Mayer Samuel Weiss resonates loudly in Houdini's life because his father had at one time been a success, an educated man—"cultured," according to the Appleton newspaper. The son boasted of the father's attainments, claiming that he "had been one of the earliest rabbis in the middle west, a Talmudic scholar of note, and a writer of speculative disquisitions." Houdini was a compulsive exaggerator (he conferred on his father a PhD and an LLD, degrees Rabbi Weiss almost certainly never earned) and a serial prevaricator (he told a British newspaper, "A whole generation of my ancestors were locksmiths"). But there's a factual basis for at least some of his claims about his father. Born and raised near Lake Balaton in western Hungary, Mayer Samuel Weisz (the spelling was later Americanized) trained to be a rabbi and was ordained in 1851, age twenty-two. No record has been found

of an association with a particular synagogue, and he seems to have taken up the profession of soapmaker, not uncommon in rabbinical families. He married, had a son, lost his wife in childbirth, and married again, in 1863, this time to Cecilia Steiner, Ehrich's beloved mother. Cecilia gave birth to four sons in the space of six years. Sometime in the late 1860s (after the dramatic relaxation of statutes limiting the activities of Hungarian Jews), Weisz began studying law at the University of Pest. On the birth certificates of the sons born in 1872, 1874, and 1876, he listed his occupation as legal counselor, which could imply that he held a comfortable position in the Civil Service.

And yet he left Hungary, leaving behind his wife and children. We don't know why, and in the absence of facts, legend holds sway. The Weiss family liked to tell the story of a duel fought over an anti-Semitic slur, a duel in which a nobleman (a prince!) died from his wounds. The victor fled to London and then to America. His family caught up with him two years later, whereupon they all settled in the Midwest.

We also don't know what Mayer Samuel Weiss was up to during his two years alone in America, or how exactly he ended up in a northern Wisconsin mill town. Although an unlikely destination, Appleton, with a population of eight thousand, was at least prospering, thanks mainly to its paper mills. Its fifteen Jewish families were raising money to build a synagogue, and for the time being services were held on the second floor of a commercial building on College Avenue. Rabbi Weiss earned a healthy salary of $750 a year, but evidently wasn't part of his congregation's plans for the future. He was too old and too attached to his Old World ways. He spoke no English—only the German of the Hapsburg Empire, as well as Hebrew and Hungarian. However proud of his distinguished scholarly bearing, the Appleton congregation seems to have preferred a younger model, one capable of assimilation.

Suddenly unemployed, with his wife Cecilia and now seven children to care for, he left Appleton for Milwaukee, a booming city on the shores of Lake Michigan with a diverse population of more than one hundred thousand, including some five hundred Jewish families. The Weiss family lived at first in a small but comfortable house (it's possible that a severance payment kept hardship and hunger at bay for a while), but soon they were moving from one tenement to the next, just a step ahead of a landlord demanding unpaid rent. Unable to find employment at any of the city's synagogues, Rabbi Weiss offered his service as a *mohel* performing ritual circumcision on Jewish infants; he also worked as a kosher butcher. And still his family's poverty was grueling. Cecilia had to rely on the charity of Milwaukee's Hebrew Relief Society, which donated a half ton of coal to keep her children warm and petty cash to keep them fed. Milwaukee was a bubbling pot into which her stubbornly unassimilated husband would or could not melt.

Mayer Samuel Weiss belonged to the Old World. Although he'd emigrated, he carried within him the oppression of a stratified, segregated society, a race memory of latent and actual violence, of exclusion and derision. The idea that this beaten man had fought a duel with a prince is preposterous, whereas the idea that he'd suffered intolerable anti-Semitic abuse is all too believable. He'd escaped the bloody pogroms and the laws that regulated where he could live and what work he could do. But in bustling Milwaukee the Weiss parents discovered that New World freedom included the freedom to fail. The exuberant promise of this new country was meant not for them but for the children.

Their eight-year-old son Ehrich landed the American boy's archetypal urban job: flogging the evening paper as a newsboy for the *Milwaukee Journal*. He also worked as a shoeshine boy. School seems not to have figured in his daily schedule. Nonetheless, he had grand ambitions. When he was nine, he performed for the first time in public, as a trapeze artist and contortionist in a youngsters' circus act. His stage name for the occasion was Ehrich, the Prince of the Air.

In 1885, his family's tragedy took another grim turn: the oldest son, Ehrich's half brother, Herman, died of tuberculosis. The mourning, the hardship, the hunger, the taint of failure were apparently too much for Ehrich to bear. He ran away. The twelve-year-old sent a postcard to his mother announcing that his aim was to reach Galveston, Texas, and that he planned to be "home in about a year." He signed the card, "your truant

son." Despite his grand ambitions, he got only as far as Kansas City, Missouri, then somehow found himself back in Wisconsin, in Delavan, about fifty miles southwest of Milwaukee. A small town set in gently rolling farmland, Delavan was the winter home of a number of traveling circuses. (The circus was then at the height of its popularity; the big top was the principal form of public entertainment in small-town America.) If young Ehrich was drawn to Delavan because he yearned to fly again as the Prince of the Air, he mistimed his jump. A kindly couple found him shining shoes in the downtown area, going by a new name, translated from the German: Erich White. Having discovered that he was homeless, a runaway, the couple took him in; he stayed with them for several months.

When Rabbi Weiss traded poverty in Milwaukee for poverty in New York City, Ehrich was the first member of the family to join him. Father and son roomed together in a boarding house on the Upper East Side for the final months of 1887. Cecilia and the other children made their way to Manhattan soon thereafter; reunited, the family rented a cold-water flat in the same neighborhood, on East 75th Street. Although more and more Jews were arriving in the city, demand for teachers of the Torah was not keeping pace. None of the synagogues was in need of a rabbi nearly sixty years old who had failed in the Midwest and after nine years in America still spoke no English. He had cards printed up advertising "all religious Services a Specialty" and expressing his willingness to perform the essential rites ("Marriages and Funerals, also practical MOHEL"), but never drummed up much business. He was forced to sell some of his precious books, a fine set of the *Code of Maimonides*, which was bought by a rabbi at a nearby synagogue, Bernard Drachman (who also bar mitzvahed young Ehrich). Eventually the Reverend Doctor Weiss went to work, like so many Jewish immigrants, in the rag trade, cutting linings for a necktie manufacturer. Ehrich found work in the same sweatshop, toiling away for two and a half years as an assistant lining cutter. (His employers found him "honest and industrious," like every Horatio Alger hero.)

After five years in New York, at the age of sixty-three, Mayer Samuel Weiss died following an operation for cancer of the tongue. Houdini's account of his father's death is rich in pathos and probably not reliable. As he tells it, the dying rabbi called his son Ehrich to his side and reminded him of a promise extracted in the depths of their Milwaukee misery: after her husband's death Cecilia should never want for anything. (Houdini kept that promise with a fervor bordering on obsession.) When he breathed his last, Cecilia wept bitterly and wailed, "Weiss, Weiss, you've left me with your children!!! What have you done?" The youngest child was Ehrich's ten-year-old sister; there were also two brothers aged thirteen and sixteen; Ehrich, or Ehrie as he was now more often called, was eighteen.

In his early forties, having secured fame and fortune, Houdini made a pilgrimage to the New York neighborhood of the East Sixties and Seventies where the struggling Weiss family lived in a succession of dingy apartments. For a full half hour he stared at a brick building on 69th Street, the tenement where his father's life ended. He might have been pondering the rabbi's downward spiral or his own meteoritic rise. Or perhaps he was weighing up the other legacy his father bequeathed to him— not the deep-seated aversion to failure and the compulsive urge to escape but a reverence for learning. Houdini said of him, "He had reared me in the love of books." Ehrich never had much schooling; nowhere in his papers is there such a thing as a high school diploma. Spelling and grammar were always a challenge for him, and he wrote (when there was no ghost-writer at hand) with the awkward pomposity of an imperfectly polished autodidact. Yet he became a passionate bibliophile, an avid reader as well as a collector. Among the thousands and thousands of books he acquired with the money earned as an "American self-liberator," the most significant may be the *Code of Maimonides*, the precious volumes of rabbinical literature sold by his father and subsequently returned by Rabbi Drachman in exchange for a $500 donation to his synagogue. Houdini asked for them specifically: he wanted them back as a memorial to his father.

* * *

Young Ehrie mapped his escape from the cramped immigrant world of windowless flats in dilapidated tenements long before he had the necessary tools to set himself free. Show business would be his ticket out of poverty: he would become an entertainer. This was a clearly marked path for impoverished young Jews hoping to assimilate and become "American." At the height of World War I, when he helped organize the Rabbis' Sons' Benevolent Association to raise money for the Red Cross, he was elected president, Al Jolson vice president, and Irving Berlin secretary. As Houdini told the *New York Times*, "It is surprising how many sons of Jewish clergymen there are on the stage." Indeed, the list of rabbis' and cantors' sons who made their names in show business stretches from Gershwin to Zukor. Many, like Jolson, Berlin, and Houdini, all three of the Shubert brothers and three of the four Warner brothers, were born in eastern Europe, arrived in America as children, and started their careers from scratch, without friends or influence. All were part of an explosion of immigrant talent and energy that helped define the American dream and shape American culture.

Entertainment was the way up and out. As Minnie Marx famously explained when asked why she sent her sons into show business: "Where else can people who don't know anything make so much money?" The only question was what kind of show Ehrie would put on. In Appleton he had seen his first trapeze artist, in Milwaukee his first magician; while still a boy in the Midwest he bought or was given a box of magic tricks. Though enthusiastic about conjuring and circus acts, he was also drawn to athletics, especially swimming, boxing, and running, and for a while he may have hoped to become a champion sportsman. He was fanatical about physical fitness, never smoking or drinking, and exercised rigorously. He believed that if he hadn't fallen ill, he would have won the 115-pound boxing title at the newly formed Amateur Athletic Union. In September 1890, age sixteen, he came first in a one-mile running race sponsored by the AAU.

At around the same time Ehrie discovered that one of his coworkers on the cutting bench, Jacob Hyman, a skinny kid with a mustache, was also a magic enthusiast. They practiced tricks together and dared each other to perform in public. Calling himself Eric the Great, Ehrie gave his first magic show at a neighborhood venue, the Pastime Athletic Club on East 69th Street.

The deciding influence on his teenage years was a Frenchman who had died two decades earlier: Jean-Eugène Robert-Houdin (1805–71), a great conjuror widely regarded then and now as the first modern magician. Ehrie acquired a second-hand copy of Robert-Houdin's memoirs, a volume that became his "textbook and . . . gospel," while Robert-Houdin became his "guide and hero." From that moment on, there was no doubt about what kind of entertainment Ehrie would offer the waiting world: magic would be his medium. His name henceforth was Houdini—he had been told, probably by Hyman, that a terminal "i" meant *like*, so that *Houdini* meant *Houdin-like*. Ehrie became Harry, solidly American to counterbalance the exotic surname. When he and Jacob Hyman started performing together in public, in 1891, they were the Brothers Houdini. Their few appearances in and around New York City earned just enough to persuade Harry that he could quit his garment district job.

When Hyman went his own way, Harry drafted his younger brother Theodore ("Dash") Weiss, who later achieved considerable success as a Houdini imitator, working (occasionally with Harry) under the name Hardeen. For a couple of years these flesh-and-blood Brothers Houdini toured the Northeast and Midwest, playing every kind of low-rent venue, from dime museums and medicine shows to beer halls and cheap variety theaters, often in the company of a circus troupe, blackface minstrels, snake charmers, strongmen, belly dancers, and assorted sideshow freaks. In the summer of 1893, Harry and Dash made their way to Chicago for the great World's Fair: Columbian Exposition. On the midway adjacent to the Exposition, on fairgrounds set aside for amusements, not far from the original Ferris wheel, they staged their show, billing themselves as Modern Monarchs of Mystery. Their magic, consisting of sleight of hand, card tricks, mind reading, and rope tie escapes, was capped by a grand finale, a substitution trick called the Metamorphosis.

This act was by no means the exclusive property of the Brothers Houdini, but they presented it well. They brought onstage a series of items: a trunk, which members of the audience were invited to inspect; a large cabinet with a curtained front, what Houdini called his "ghost house"; a length of rope; a black cloth sack; a tin of sealing wax. The shorter Houdini (Harry) climbed into the sack with his hands tied behind his back, the rope sealed with wax. Harry was then locked into the trunk, which was rolled into the ghost house. The taller Houdini (Dash) stepped behind the crimson curtain and clapped his hands once, twice, thrice—and presto!—the curtain was thrown open from the inside by Harry, who had seconds before been trussed up and locked away. The astonished audience gaped as the trunk was now opened to reveal that the brothers had swapped places: Dash was in the black sack, hands tied, sealing wax intact. Monarchs of mystery indeed!

The partnership between Harry and Dash dissolved abruptly with another rapid and mysterious substitution: on June 22, 1894, a year after the gig at the World's Fair, Harry married—almost as soon as he met her—a young performer who replaced his acquiescent brother. The new act bore a new name; Mr. and Mrs. Harry Houdini performed as the Great Houdinis.

2

From Dime Museums to Vaudeville

FROM HIS PREHENSILE TOES to the thick curly dark hair on the top of his unusually large head, Houdini measured five foot four. He was small and compact, intensely muscular, flexible as well as strong, with a broad chest and a handsome face. His long, straight nose, prominent upper lip, and bold cleft chin gave him an assertive look. Except that he was slightly bow-legged and less than average height, he was a perfect specimen—male anatomy in its ideal form. The critic Edmund Wilson remarked on the "dignity and force" of the magician's outsized head: "Wide-browed and aquiline nosed," Houdini reminded Wilson of "one of those enlarged and idealized busts of Roman generals or consuls." Others called him "magnetic," a tribute to his charisma and also to his impressive physique.

His bride, Wilhelmina Beatrice ("Bess") Rahner, just eighteen when they married, was tiny—four foot nine—and looked like a dainty version of her husband, with the same long straight nose, same prominent upper lip. (Her chin, however, was not cleft.) She could have been his younger sister. She had recently joined a song-and-dance group called the Floral Sisters who were performing, as was Harry, in Coney Island, already a vast adult playground, with its resort beaches, racetracks, roller coasters, dance halls, and casinos. It's possible that Harry and Bess saw one another perform onstage before they met face-to-face. In any case, three weeks after their first encounter they were married in a civil ceremony. Bess was from Brooklyn, a Roman Catholic girl; although Cecilia Weiss welcomed Bess into the family, Bess's widowed mother, a German immigrant, refused to meet her Jewish son-in-law. In the eyes of the widow Rahner, "a Jew was a person of doubtful human attributes." It would be a dozen years before Houdini's mother-in-law was reconciled to his existence.

The Great Houdinis were a new, improved version of the Brothers Houdini. The young Mrs. Houdini was an ideal replacement for Dash: Harry (Monsieur) was a commanding presence next to Bess (Mademoiselle, despite her marital status). Her size and sex gave Metamorphosis an edge it had previously lacked. At the beginning of the act Monsieur allowed himself to be confined and concealed; he ended it triumphant, liberated, his diminutive double in the sack, secured and subjugated. The female captive, the male unbound. Or, perhaps more confusingly, a bound male morphed into a bound female. Mademoiselle often wore a Little Lord Fauntleroy suit (black knickerbockers, white shirt, rounded collar), an outfit that blurred the line between boy and girl. Either way, the double act was thrilling. It was magic.

Or not. Usually unmasking magic leads to disappointment—take away the mystery and the monarchs look sadly like commoners—but in the case of Metamorphosis, the secret of the trick can be revealed without diminishing the spectacle or impugning the couple's prowess. What happened behind the

crimson curtain of the ghost house? From the outside the trunk on wheels (known in the trade as a substitution trunk, or "sub trunk") appeared sound, but a back panel swung inward if you knew exactly where to press a catch concealed on the inside. The black sack was slit at the bottom. The rope tie was no obstacle to an adept conjuror. Still, the Houdinis achieved the substitution in only three seconds, an astounding feat of agility and showmanship. A contemporary newspaper account noted admiringly that the switch occurred "as quickly as one can fire a self-cocking pistol." It helped, of course, that Bess was miniscule and nimble, and that the preternaturally agile Harry was also conspicuously theatrical, with a hint of a mid-European accent made more exotic by the staccato rhythm of his onstage patter. He had a wide, persuasive smile.

Metamorphosis was the catalyst that eventually transformed his career, and the illusion remained in the Houdini repertoire for decades—but for now the longed-for breakthrough proved elusive. Harry and Bess toiled away in obscurity for more than five years, touring ceaselessly, traveling to Podunk towns where they performed a dozen times a day, or even twenty times a day, often on cramped makeshift stages in front of drunken, bored, or hostile audiences, earning barely enough to keep themselves alive. On more than one occasion the venue was simply too squalid, and they walked away without performing. But they needed to earn a wage, and so endured the indignities as best they could.

These arduous early years on the road forged a deep and lasting bond between husband and wife. Married for more than three decades, Harry and Bess were parted only by Harry's death. The conjugal bond endured partly because it began as an effective working partnership. Professional convenience and pragmatism played a role, and may even have provided the spark: ambition may have pushed Harry into marrying. And yet the mood of the marriage was hardly businesslike. From the beginning, Harry felt it necessary to dress up the union with all kinds of elaborate romantic frills: poetic declarations of undying love, saccharine endearments, cooing notes left on his wife's pillow or the kitchen counter.

Adorable
Sunshine

of my Life,
I have had my coffee,
    have washed out this glass,
    and am on my way to business.
Houdini
"My darling I love you."

Other notes were addressed to "BEAUTIFUL BEATRICE HOUDINI"
or "Darling-Darling Darling" or "Honey-Baby-Pretty-Lamby";
one was signed "a trillion, billion Kadillion million, Kisses sin-
cerely the rube who is stuck on you." For all those many kisses,
the passion proclaimed was not erotic; it was lovey-dovey.
Harry was a prude when it came to sex—scandalized by prosti-
tution and, when he began making movies, squeamish about
kissing starlets on set. "I'm afraid I'm not much of a ladies'
man," he told a reporter.

Although he had acquired a wife, his mother remained paramount in his affections. As Bess graciously put it, "There were
of course two loves in his life, running parallel, so to speak."
Harry was not a ladies' man but, as he frankly confessed, "I am
what would be called a Mothers-boy." To anyone but her son,
Cecilia seemed an unremarkable woman; to Harry she was a
paragon, the peerless epitome of motherhood. After nearly
twenty years of marriage he was still insisting to his spouse that
his devotion to his mother was not only inevitable but appro-
priate: "I love you as I shall never again love any woman, but
the love for a mother is a love that only a true mother ought to
possess, for she loved me before I was born and naturally will
love me until one or the other passes away into the Great Beyond, not passing away but simply let us say 'gone on ahead.'"

Marrying Bess at age twenty was a sign of confidence in his
future, but that confidence needed bolstering. According to
Bess, after the wedding, on the night of the last performance by
the Brothers Houdini, Harry asked that she and Dash take a

walk with him into the countryside around Coney Island. On a "dark lonely bridge" Harry asked them to swear a solemn oath of loyalty: "Never betray me in any way, so help you God." She kept that vow, remaining steadfast for more than three decades, and after his death looked back with reverent fondness on their marriage and spoke of Harry's "unfailing tenderness" with her.

They had no children. "God has seen fit not to Bless Bess and myself with children," he wrote, "even though Ma prayed for it." The absence of progeny has given rise to elaborate speculation and rumor. It's been argued, unconvincingly, that Harry was impotent. Hearsay evidence suggests that Bess was afflicted with primary amenorrhea—she simply never menstruated. (Her niece claimed to have heard her say so.) Despite their disappointment, Harry and Bess were still hoping to become parents a decade after their wedding. "My wife says she wishes she could raise children and stop working," Houdini wrote to a friend in 1903, "and perhaps in 1905 we may rest long enough to raise one of them things called children ourselves."

They had pets instead. Charlie, a white Pomeranian, toured Europe with them. When Charlie died he was replaced by Bobby, a fox terrier adept at turning somersaults. The Houdinis also had a "dream child," a fantasy son named Mayer Samuel after Harry's father. Harry wrote about the boy's exploits in letters and notes to Bess. Eventually Mayer Samuel became president of the United States—at which point the letters cease.

Harry liked Bess to mother him. He relied on her to wash his ears for him, to make sure he wore clean clothes, to cook his meals on the rare occasions when he was home. The year he died—when he was a fifty-two years old—his character was impugned in front of a congressional subcommittee weighing the merits of a bill banning fortune-telling in the District of Columbia. To clear his name, he called upon Bess to vouch for him, bringing her forward to testify with theatrical flair that drew laughter from the audience:

> HOUDINI: Step this way Mrs. Houdini. One of the witnesses said I was a brute and that I was vile and I was crazy. Won't you step this way? I want the chairman to see you. I will have been married on June 22nd, 32 years to this girl. . . . There are no medals and no ribbons on me, but when a girl will stick to a man for 32 years as she did and when she will starve with me and work with me through thick and thin, it is a pretty good recommendation. Outside of my great mother, Mrs. Houdini has been my greatest friend. [To Mrs. Houdini] Have I shown traces of being crazy, unless it was about you?
>   [More laughter from the audience.]
>   MRS. HOUDINI: No.
>   HOUDINI: Am I brutal to you or vile?
>   MRS. HOUDINI: No.
>   HOUDINI: Am I good boy?
>   MRS. HOUDINI: Yes.
>   HOUDINI: Thank you Mrs. Houdini.
>   [The audience applauds.]

He *was* a good boy—except when he wasn't. He was wary of displeasing Bess, who was "quick-tempered" and occasionally sulked and in her later years drank too much. In his journal he often mentioned her mood, especially when she was "sore" with him or having an attack of "nerves." In a love note addressed to "Honey lamb, sweetheart," he told her, "Even though you do get a 'tantrum' and give me hell, I'd rather have you with me." Harry never drank or smoked, but he did get the urge to gamble. After his first consequential loss ($60 in a crap game), he promised Bess that it would never happen again, and it never did. He had at least one extramarital affair; if Bess had an affair, it remains secret. It was evidently important to Harry that his marriage seem to others—to the "audience"—ideal. As far as he was concerned, it mostly was.

*   *   *

In the summer of 1895, a year after they were married, Harry and Bess joined forces for a few months with the Welsh Brothers Circus Troupe, which at the time operated mostly in Pennsylvania. For $25 a week, the Houdinis did it all, every kind of big-top entertainment, from hypnotism to clowning to song and dance to acrobatics. Harry even agreed to appear as a sideshow freak, Projea, the Wild Man of Mexico; he turned himself into a snarling caveman creature who hurled himself at the bars of his cage and gnawed at chunks of raw meat.

He later claimed to have learned a great deal from sideshow freaks and other circus hands. Befriending a fat lady, a strongman, an armless wonder who played the violin with his toes, a woman impervious to pain, Houdini picked up tricks of the trade. From a Japanese acrobat he learned a swallowing technique that led him, eventually, to one of his signature acts. From the armless man he learned how to articulate his toes. He studied showmanship, so often the difference between a successful act and a flop. He saw firsthand the practical application of a lesson imparted by Robert-Houdin: "A conjurer . . . is an *actor* playing the role of a magician." To the uninitiated, it might seem that freaks were freaks, that all they had to do in order to excite curiosity (and that queasy amalgam of fear, loathing, and voyeuristic thrill) was to display themselves to the public. But the best freaks *performed*, dramatizing their singularity, sometimes subtly, sometimes not. Perhaps the most profound lesson Houdini learned from the "curio stage" was to recognize his own marginal status. His Jewishness set him apart (if only because it made him so intent on assimilation, so insistent on being American), but circus freaks revealed to him a different kind of liminality. Especially in these early years, but also after he became a celebrity, Harry tacitly accepted that he was different—

perhaps not a Wild Man of Mexico, but nonetheless an out-
sider, separated from the world of ordinary men and women by
his talent and untamed ambition. He once told a reporter from
the London *Times* that he felt more comfortable "with strong-
arm men and bear wrestlers" than with "Blue-Bloods." Circus
freaks were his kind of people.

In September 1895, a cousin on his mother's side convinced
him to buy a 50 percent stake in a traveling burlesque show, the
American Gaiety Girls. That Houdini—who was viscerally re-
pelled by anything smutty—would agree to associate himself
with a show that could prosper only by baring female flesh,
belting out bawdy songs, and winking at vulgar jokes tells us
how desperate he was for success. Newly married and still only

twenty-one, he was willing to try anything. Yet this particular gamble did not pay off. Decades later he boasted that the troupe was "the finest, cleanest, and largest show of its kind on the road that season"—but the appeal of burlesque necessarily involves peddling erotic fantasy. One of the fine, clean acts featured a female wrestler ready to challenge any woman—or any man weighing less than 122 pounds. The rapid demise of the venture was surely a blessing in disguise.

It was while Houdini was managing the American Gaiety Girls that he first added handcuffs to his repertoire. He bought a ring of handcuff keys and worked with them tirelessly until he was adept enough to perform in public. One night in November 1895, in Manchester, New Hampshire, as he prepared for Metamorphosis, he offered to have his hands secured not with ropes but with cuffs supplied by a member of the audience. Hoping to publicize this novel aspect of his routine, he presented himself at the police station of the next town they visited (Gloucester, Massachusetts) and showed off his new skill, telling the officers that he could escape from any make of handcuff. The *Gloucester Daily Times* covered the stunt in its news section—and closed the item by noting that Houdini would be performing onstage that evening. A few days later, under the jaundiced eyes of the Woonsocket, Rhode Island, police force, Houdini escaped from a half dozen different pairs at once, including an elaborate set that required a separate key for each hand. The routine was always the same: once shackled, Houdini stepped into the next room and in less than a minute emerged with his arms unencumbered. The Woonsocket newspaper ran a story, complete with photo; the headline was "Handcuffs Don't Count." In Holyoke, Massachusetts, the *Daily Democrat* reported that Houdini shed handcuffs "as if they were strings wound round his wrists."

The free publicity failed to keep the American Gaiety Girls afloat. But Harry persisted with his visits to local lock-ups, certain that sooner or later the police and the press would combine to generate the kind of attention success required.

After their brief, unprofitable burlesque detour, Harry and Bess signed up in the spring of 1896 for a tour of Canada's Maritime Provinces with a magic show called the Marco Company. Harry hadn't left the United States since he'd arrived at Castle Garden, the precursor to Ellis Island, at the age of four with his mother and siblings aboard the SS *Frisia*. Now he was booked on a steamship sailing from Boston to Yarmouth, Nova Scotia. The moment he stepped onto the gangway, he felt queasy; on deck, once the boat began to move, he felt worse; by the time they were out in the open water of the Gulf of Maine, he was clutching the rail in misery, retching into the water below. Seasickness plagued him all his life. On a moving boat, the eerie control over his body that allowed him to perform his escapes failed entirely—he was almost always desperately ill for the length of the passage.

A Nova Scotia native, Edward J. Dooley, aka Marco, the Monarch of Mystery and the owner of the Marco Company, was a talented musician who earned his living as church organist and choirmaster. He was also an amateur magician who dreamed of becoming a professional. Unfortunately, he was neither a talented conjuror nor an efficient manager, and his company went bust barely a month after arriving in Canada, having played to empty houses in various small cities in Nova Scotia and New Brunswick. Though ineffectual, Dooley was a kind man. Onstage, he presented Bess as his daughter (Mademoiselle Marco) and Harry as his son-in-law and "successor." This little family fell apart when a sheriff in Halifax interrupted a performance to seize the company's apparatus on behalf of creditors.

The Canada tour wasn't a complete disaster. In New Brunswick Houdini added a new escape that became one of his signature acts. The chief of police in the port city of Saint John was eager to test a "maniac cuff and belt" consisting of a stiff leather mitten and a long leather belt. Both hands were placed in the mitten, wrists locked together, and a leather belt wound tight around the forearms and then the waist—a challenge, certainly (Harry had to hold the key in his teeth to unlock the cuffs), but not a device that could hold Houdini, the self-crowned Handcuff King. The Saint John police chief was related by marriage to the superintendent of the nearby New Brunswick Provincial Lunatic Asylum, a hilltop institution that housed some six hundred patients; the chief suggested that Houdini pay a visit. As part of the tour Houdini was shown the padded cells. Through the bars of one door he watched an inmate struggling on the floor, desperately trying to free himself from a canvas restraint. Fascinated by the poor man's exertions, Houdini asked the name of the restraining device and was told it was a strait-jacket; he then of course asked to borrow one. For the next week he spent all his free time perfecting a technique for shedding the restraint. (Houdini's early onstage straitjacket escapes were accomplished behind a curtain or screen. It wasn't until several years later, following his brother Theo's lead, that he attempted the feat in full view of an audience. Only in 1915, nearly two decades after the Canada tour, did Houdini start performing *suspended* straitjacket escapes, dangling upside down, high above streets crammed with spectators.)

It was in Halifax, Nova Scotia, in June 1896, a week before the abrupt dissolution of the Marco Company, that Houdini performed his first jailbreak. The municipal prison, housed in the basement of the city hall, was modern and secure. The fifteen cells reserved for male prisoners each measured four foot by seven; the brick walls were nearly a foot thick, the doors made of heavy iron. Houdini presented himself at this formidable lock-up fully clothed; he then stripped down to a bathing suit to show that he wasn't hiding any tools. The officers handcuffed him, locked him in one cell, locked his clothes in another, and went about their business. They discovered that he had escaped only when the concierge of the Queen Hotel telephoned to ask that Houdini's clothes be sent over to his room. The pattern was thereby set for publicity stunts in city after city—the jailbreak became one of his favorite tricks.

Toward the end of 1897 the Houdinis found several months of steady work touring the Midwest with the California Concert Company, a medicine show run by a slick character who called himself "Dr." Thomas Hill and peddled a patent medicine he claimed could cure just about any ailment under the sun. Among the company's performers was a husband-and-wife vaudeville act called the Keatons who befriended Harry and Bess. The Keatons had a toddler who would grow up to be the silent film star Buster Keaton. Both Harry and Buster later declared that it was Harry who gave the boy his nickname. The toddler took a tumble down some stairs and shrugged it off; impressed, Harry exclaimed, "That was a real buster!" In those days, Keaton reported, a "buster" was a potentially harmful spill. (A suspiciously tidy anecdote, especially considering that one of Keaton's specialties was the pratfall stoically endured.)

In the spring of 1898 Harry and Bess (or Mysterious Harry and La Petite Bessie, as they often billed themselves) joined up with the Welsh Brothers for a second tour, a six-month spell that ended when the circus closed for the season at the beginning of October. Near the end of this return engagement Houdini began training as an acrobat, practicing somersaults—double, front and back—and performing alongside the Bard Brothers, circus gymnasts. He even bought a costume: "pink tights and uppers."

Burlesque and acrobatics weren't the only sidelines the Houdinis explored during the hungry years. Borrowing Bessie's maiden name, they appeared as the Rahners, a comedy duo. For a brief while Harry called himself Cardo and presented an evening of card tricks. As Professor Murat, he turned hypnotist, putting Bess in a trance, a sham quickly dropped from their repertory. And for a few months, during and after their stint with Dr. Hill's medicine show, they toured as mediums conducting Spiritualist séances.

Spiritualism American-style announced its birth in the late 1840s with a series of mysterious knocks and raps in a farmhouse in Hydesville, New York, restless spirits making themselves known to a pair of teenage sisters, Margaret and Kate Fox (who admitted forty years later that it was all a hoax). In the last several decades of the nineteenth century, in the wake of Civil War carnage, Spiritualism spread across the country and enjoyed vast popularity as a loosely connected set of beliefs all centered on the tenet that communication was possible between the living and the dead. This possibility aroused intense curiosity and tantalizing hope in those who yearned to believe in an afterlife. Spirit mediums who promised to put the bereaved in contact with the dearly departed thrived in this hopeful (and credulous) environment, as did magicians who suggested that their illusions were manifestations of the supernatural. The most famous of these were William and Ira Davenport, who were neither mediums nor conventional magicians but something in between. The Davenport Brothers' act, which Houdini admired immensely, was in some ways the opposite of what he himself did: instead of escaping, they pretended *not* to escape. In a séance setting, they were tied up securely and lashed to their seats inside a large wooden cabinet in which certain musical instruments were hung on hooks, out of reach. As soon as the cabinet doors were closed, the instruments would sound, a strumming guitar, a recorder, a tambourine, a ringing bell—a cacophony of sound. When the doors were reopened, the somber, mustachioed brothers would be still be tied up tight, leaving the audience to surmise that spirits summoned by the Davenports had been making the mystery music. These brothers, from Buffalo, New York, created a sensation in the 1850s and '60s, touring in the United States and in Europe, performing for the queen of England, the emperor of France, the tsar of Russia.

As for Harry and Bess, they'd been performing a mind-reading act for several years, though not in front of royalty. In addition to their other skills, they sometimes claimed to be "Occult Expositors." Bess would sit center stage, blindfolded, while Houdini circulated in the audience asking people in the crowd to show him a coin out of their pocket; he asked them to examine the date on the coin (making sure to get a glimpse of it himself), hold the coin tight, and concentrate on the date. Mademoiselle Houdini would then read their minds and recite the correct years. (The trick relied on coded communication between magician and mind-reader: key words in his patter stood for numbers between one and ten.)

The act they began presenting with the California Concert Company, a "spiritualistic séance," required more sophisticated preparation. Billing themselves as Prof. Harry Houdini, the Great Mystifier, and Mlle. Beatrice Houdini, the Celebrated Psycrometic Clairvoyant, they offered to make "spiritual forms" materialize, to make tables and musical instruments float in midair, and—if conditions were right—transmit messages from the dead.

To craft those messages, they did some sleuthing upon their arrival in any new town. They would visit the cemetery to examine the inscriptions on gravestones, chat with the sexton or with loose-tongued locals in the barbershop, and—if they could manage it—sneak a peek at someone's family Bible. Mostly they were searching for names and dates, births and deaths, but scandal played well, too—an unsolved murder or rumored hanky-panky. When it became clear that the séances were boosting the profits of the medicine show, Houdini began consulting what was known in the trade as "The Blue Book," a repository of information shared by mediums about the clients who attended séances. Armed with fragments of local knowledge, Professor and Mademoiselle Houdini were ready to commune with the spirits on behalf of the townsfolk. He would put her in a trance, or vice versa—and to the astonishment of the audience, the medium would begin to spout a few trifles about prominent families, dredge up some gossip, or hint at notorious neighborhood indiscretions. The trick was to deploy just enough fact to let innuendo and supposition do the bulk of the work. The effect on their public was electrifying; word spread, and soon they were playing to packed houses. "To me it was a lark," Houdini later wrote. "I was a mystifier and as such my ambition was being gratified and my love for a mild sensation satisfied."

When Harry and Bess parted company with Dr. Hill, they carried on with the séances, and for the first time in their show business career, began to feel flush—"lived like a king," Harry wrote in his journal. But suddenly he and Bessie gave it up. Even as he was calculating the financial benefits of posing as a spirit medium, noting in his journal that in Galena, Kansas, he'd raked in $700 with eight shows, or that more than a thousand people (a record for Garnett, Kansas) "paid admission to see spiritualism," he confessed that it was a "Bad effect."

Their success as spirit mediums was too conspicuous for them to be comfortable with it. They couldn't avoid the conclusion that it depended less on their skill than on the spiritual hunger of the desperately eager crowds that filled the theaters. As Houdini wrote many years later, "I saw and felt that the audience believed in me . . . they believed that my tricks were true communications from the dead. I was brought to a realization of the seriousness of trifling with the hallowed reverence which the average human being bestows on the departed. . . . I was chagrined that I should ever have been guilty of such frivolity and for the first time I realized that it bordered on crime." This mea culpa was composed decades later, after he'd embarked on his famous crusade against phony mediums; though surely sincere, it was also part of a rhetorical strategy: the confession was intended to expose the humbug peddled by others. And there can be no doubting the sincerity of Harry's feelings about mourning, especially after the death of his mother in 1913. His grief became as important to him as Cecilia had been. Spirit mediums who dishonored the dead with their fakery roused a fury in him.

Honesty was not usually his policy. Any untruth in the service of publicity was perfectly acceptable to him, as was any deception in the service of illusions performed onstage. As a struggling magician, he had no compunction about printing a playbill advertising Metamorphosis as an act the Houdinis had performed in Paris and in London (at the Egyptian Hall in Piccadilly, no less), when in fact they had not yet set foot in England. Boasting to a reporter about his international stardom on a visit to Appleton in 1897 (when Canada was the only foreign country he'd toured) was a simple matter of self-promotion— but Harry went further, insisting that he had "studied and practiced for a considerable time in London." Lying about the apparatus used in a trick was also fair play—even though the untruth might lead the gullible to conclude that the Houdinis possessed supernatural powers. If the ethical line between promotional falsehood and a conjuror's deception on the one hand and the "crime" of a charlatan spirit medium on the other seems from this distance somewhat hazy, Houdini was convinced he knew where it lay.

Back in New York City after their second tour with the Welsh Brothers, they stayed with Harry's beloved mother—her apartment on East 69th Street was the closest thing they had to a home. Whatever troupe they were traveling with, whatever one-horse town they were playing in, and however poor their pay packet, there was one ritual they never neglected: sending a portion of their weekly earnings, if any, back to Cecilia Weiss. Harry had a promise to honor—his mother must never want

for anything. Even if he failed in his attempt to escape his father's fate by becoming a show business star, his mother must
never suffer.

And failure, by the end of 1898, was a distinct possibility.
The Houdinis were seemingly incapable of making a good living without the assistance of the supernatural. Though Harry
sent out flyers to theater managers hoping for bookings in the
new year, he and Bess were tempted to quit. Harry compiled a
sixteen-page catalogue of his tricks, offering to sell his secrets—
even Metamorphosis and his handcuff escapes ("Price on application"). There were no takers. On the back of the catalogue
was an advertisement for Professor Harry Houdini's School
of Magic. No students enrolled. When new bookings came
through, they went back on the road, the only life they'd known
together.

In Chicago in the closing months of 1898, Houdini worked
hard for free publicity from the police force, and was rewarded
with a dream endorsement. He befriended a detective named
Andrew Rohan who arranged a demonstration of Houdini's
prowess in the roll-call room of the Central Station. Houdini
was cuffed and fitted with leg irons and then the cuffs were
manacled to the leg irons so that he had to be helped into his
escape cabinet—where he spent a couple of minutes before
emerging utterly free and presented the devices, still locked
and undamaged, to the baffled policemen. Lieutenant Rohan,
sounding more like a shill than a cop, trumpeted Houdini's talents far and wide, ably assisted by reporters from the Chicago
press. Rohan described the escape as "miraculous"; the papers
concurred.

* * *

Maybe it was dumb luck, maybe it was persistence rewarded.
In the spring of 1899, the Houdinis were playing at a beer hall
in St. Paul, Minnesota, when in walked a group of theater owners and managers scouting for talent. One of them was Martin

Beck, a powerful vaudeville impresario in charge of the Orpheum circuit, a chain of successful theaters in the West and
Midwest. Impressed with the Houdinis' performance, Beck
came back the next night and brought with him several pairs
of handcuffs with which he challenged the Handcuff King—
who escaped without breaking a sweat.

On March 14, Beck sent Houdini a telegram: "You can open
Omaha March twenty sixth sixty dollars. will see act probably
make you proposition for all next season." Harry wrote across
the bottom of the telegram, "This wire changed my whole Life's
journey."

It would be hard to exaggerate how radical the change was.
His weekly pay more than doubled, but that was the least of it.
Vaudeville—high-end vaudeville of the kind presented on the
Orpheum circuit—was both immensely popular and respect-
able in a way that medicine shows and circus troupes and burlesque companies couldn't hope to be. To sign a contract with
Beck, as Houdini did on April 27, and spend the season touring
his theaters, was to experience a degree of comfort, security,
and status Harry and Bess had never known.

No more dime museums, no more sideshow freaks, no
more beer halls and revival tents, no more one-night stands
in Nowheresville, USA—Houdini had hit the big time. Bess
reaped the benefit along with Harry, but there was no longer
any suggestion that theirs was a double act. Though she remained his assistant, and played her agile part in Metamorphosis, he was now emphatically the sole star of the act, the Great
Houdini, King of Handcuffs. In time she disappeared entirely
from the posters advertising the show, a vanishing act that
seems not to have troubled her at all.

As for Harry, it was not in his nature to become compla-
cent. Every waking hour was devoted to magic and escapology.
Straightaway he introduced a new trick, needle swallowing, a
greatly refined and elaborated version of the swallowing trick

picked up several years earlier from a Japanese circus acrobat. He would pop a set of sewing needles in his mouth, chew them loudly, swallow them, then swallow a length of thread, then pull from his mouth the thread with the needles neatly strung along it. Members of the audience came onstage to peer into his mouth each step of the way; by amplifying with their studious attention what was essentially a parlor trick, the public provided the drama that meant the trick played well in a large theater. Harry also sharpened his card act. But the main event was escape—from the Metamorphosis trunk, from handcuffs, leg irons, straitjackets. He continued to accept challenges from the audience, and advertised a monetary reward ($50) if anyone could foil him. For the first time he performed his handcuff escape in view of the audience—his back turned but the curtain of his cabinet open—and noted in his diary that it was "the hit of the act."

What special talent had Martin Beck spotted? Like Harry, Beck was a Jewish immigrant from the Austro-Hungarian Empire. Born in what is now Slovakia, he'd come to America as a sixteen-year-old with a German theater group. He made good in theater management in San Francisco after several hard penniless years in New York and Chicago. Beck wasn't interested in Houdini's magic tricks, which were not in any case performed with special flair. (As many of his fellow magicians have argued then and now, Houdini was not an especially talented conjuror.) It was the escape act that resonated with Beck— Houdini's tireless unstoppable urge to break free. Beck understood that in Houdini's act, escape equaled success. It was a drama that thrilled the audience and also offered something more than entertainment: escape, in the hands of an escape artist, became a matter of life and death.

Beck also noted with satisfaction Houdini's insatiable craving for the limelight, and his knack for finding it. He had gradually perfected his police station stunt so that press coverage of

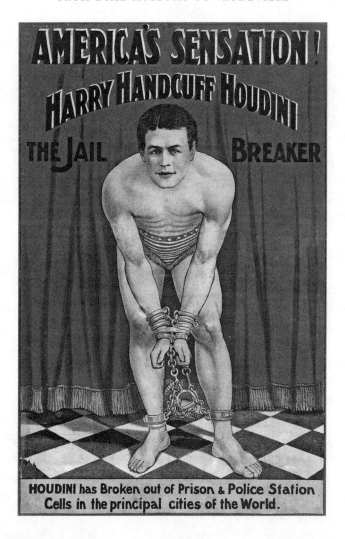

policemen scratching their heads and muttering in outrage and admiration announced his arrival in every new city. In early June in San Francisco, where he was booked for a two-week run at the Orpheum Theater, he gave a master class in escapology to an assembly of several hundred officers. Returning to the city in mid-July, he arranged another spectacle at the station.

To counter accusations that he kept keys and lock picks concealed on his person, he stripped under the watchful eyes of a crowd of cops and allowed himself to be poked and prodded by a medical examiner, who then taped shut his mouth. At last the cuffs were clamped on—ten pairs, one of which was locked onto the chain that bound his ankles. Bent nearly in half and weighed down with all that biting iron, he was picked up and deposited in a closet. He emerged five minutes later, disburdened. In Chicago in early April 1900, he raised the ante by escaping, naked, from handcuffs *and* a jail cell—a cell equipped with two locks, one of which was located beyond the prisoner's reach. The headlines were all variations on a theme: "Houdini Amazes the Detectives."

In promotional material he spelled out his claim to fame: "The only Conjurer in the World that Escapes out of all Handcuffs, Leg Shackles, Insane belts and Strait-Jackets, after being STRIPPED STARK NAKED, mouth sealed up and thoroughly searched from head to foot, proving he carries no KEYS, SPRINGS, WIRES or other concealed accessories." Or, as he put it more succinctly: "The Handcuff act can not be done searched and naked after my style by *any one on earth*." And in another advertisement, he further inflated the claim: "ONE OF THE GREATEST MAGICAL FEATS SINCE BIBLICAL TIMES." (The psychotherapist Adam Phillips, writing about Houdini's urge to be "the Napoleon of advertising," remarked, "Even if it is intended for public consumption, boasting is a curiously solitary act. More the soliloquy of the uncertain.")

Nakedness had become part of the Houdini legend: *stark naked* is the phrase most often repeated, but there was also an emphasis on the removal of *every stitch of clothing*. He did not of course appear in the buff with ladies present, yet no one, man or woman, who saw his act was unaware of his habit of disrobing in police stations, and he often appeared onstage scantily clad—in a bathing suit, for example. The focus of any Houdini

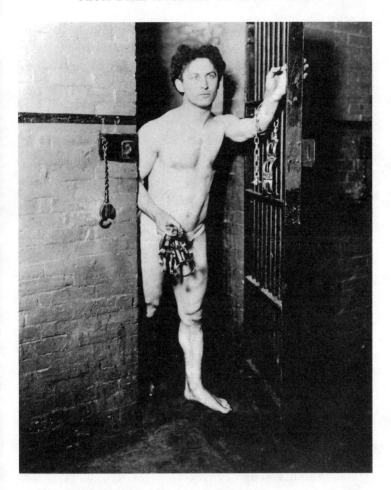

performance was on his body and its chief attributes: flexibility, strength, agility, endurance. His body was inspected onstage and subject to the indignity of restraint. He was festooned, garlanded, with chains. And then he was imprisoned—but thanks to his magnificent and mysterious body, he set himself free, a self-liberation that affirmed his masculinity.

At jailhouses all over the country, he was surrounded by uniformed officers, stripped naked, and examined by police surgeons who inspected with fingers and surgical instruments every orifice in his body. The humiliation was compounded by incarceration. The overt and implied message was that Houdini was helpless, held captive by representatives of the state, defeated, emasculated, impotent. But when he reappeared within minutes, unbound and reclothed, degradation turned to triumph. Here was a man capable of resisting the power of authority over the individual. Self-liberated, he was once again supremely masculine. Victory restored virility.

It's tempting to engage in psychosexual speculation, to hatch theories about why this prudish man invited male authority figures like policemen to scrutinize his nakedness, to poke and prod. He submitted passively to this treatment—and then confounded and defeated the authorities by breaking free from his shackles or escaping from his cell. There's no clear evidence that this bizarre ritual gave him a sexual thrill, or even satisfied a deep psychic need—except that he did it again and again. He may have liked to show off his naked body out of simple vanity, and the only way he could do so was in front of an all-male audience. Or it may be that he was doing whatever was needed to attract publicity.

Under scrutiny, his body was compared with that of Eugene Sandow, a strongman whose "muscle display performances" made him a star of the vaudeville circuit. At the time of the 1893 World's Fair in Chicago, Sandow's sensational three-month run at the Trocadero Theatre made him famous and also launched the career of the young Florenz Ziegfeld, Jr., whose advertisements proclaimed that Sandow, already touted as "the strongest man on earth," represented "the perfection of physical manhood." Sandow performed startling feats of strength and also exhibited his body near naked, as though it were a classical sculpture or a scientific curiosity. (His physique was of course the object of erotic fascination for both men and women, but that aspect of the performance was obscured by appeals to art

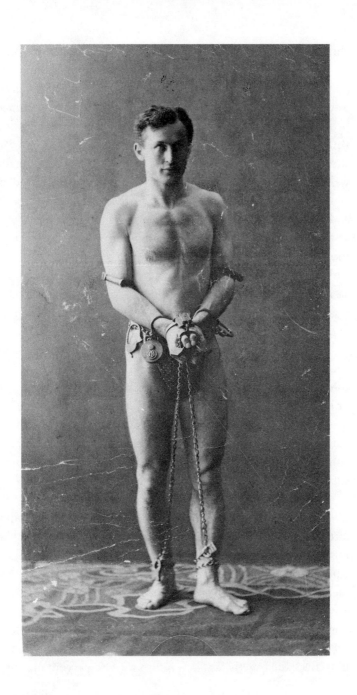

and science and to the health benefits of the exercise routines he promoted as "physical culture.") Although Houdini displayed his body only in conjunction with his escapes (it was always adorned with cuffs and manacles, or about to be confined or imprisoned), he was happy to benefit from any association with the celebrated Sandow and his "plastic poses." Harry was shorter and slighter than Sandow, but he too had unusually well-defined muscles. The *St. Louis Post-Dispatch* published an article illustrated with side-by-side photos of Harry's forearm and Sandow's under the headline "Marvelously Developed Forearm of Magician Houdini." The comparison revealed that although Sandow's forearm was bigger, Harry's wrist was smaller, which meant that the conjuror's arm muscles were proportionately larger. Did this mean that Houdini's "physical manhood" was more perfect than perfection? He was well on his way to becoming a superhero.

Houdini was not a bodybuilder (a term coined by Sandow), yet in a sense his body *was* his act. As the cultural historian John F. Kasson has remarked, "Naked or clothed, fully exposed or hidden from sight, [Houdini] made issues of the body and of masculinity central to his art." An escape artist liberates his or her body from constraint, or survives some threatened harm. After the ordeal, the unfettered, unscathed body is proof of success. The body becomes the emblem of triumph.

* * *

A year under Beck's management transformed Houdini into a highly paid headliner on the vaudeville circuit: regular raises pumped his weekly salary up to $400 (more than half of what his father had earned in a full year as the rabbi of the Appleton congregation). Beck's Orpheum circuit had a reciprocal arrangement with the Keith circuit, which controlled the major East Coast vaudeville theaters, and so Houdini also played New York, Washington, and Boston. Having promised to "boost" him, Beck did exactly that—in return for a 20 percent management fee. He boosted him to the point where performer and impresario began to clash. As though he were following a hack-neyed script, Houdini began to behave like a diva. And Beck responded predictably, pointing out that it was the manager's prestige and influence that had made possible Harry's meteoric rise. Their professional relationship never recovered, and in July 1901, Harry asked to be released from his contract.

By then Harry and Bess had turned their backs on their American success. They had made their most ambitious move yet: on May 30, 1900, they boarded the SS *Kensington* and sailed for England.

3

The Handcuff King Conquers Europe

THE CROSSING was a misery for Harry, whose seasickness was no less acute than it had been four years earlier and ended only when they docked in Southampton, on June 9. They journeyed on to London where they took lodgings on Keppel Street, Bloomsbury, a block and a half from the British Museum. Having recovered from seasickness, Harry now faced what the theater world calls "shipwreck": the Houdinis discovered that the agent who had promised them advanced bookings in Europe was "a Dam Liar"—no such bookings existed.

Harry and Bess met with several theatrical agents in London, but none of them showed interest in taking them on. Harry did however procure an introduction to C. Dundas Slater, manager of the Alhambra Theatre in Leicester Square, one of the city's grandest music halls. Unfortunately, when the Great Houdini presented himself at the Alhambra, Slater was openly scornful of handcuff escapes. There are conflicting stories about how Harry won him over. The more picturesque version has Harry—who at this point had been in London all of five days— arranging a demonstration for Slater at Scotland Yard, where Houdini was shackled to a pillar with a pair of regulation British cuffs. He shed the cuffs before you could say tea and crumpets; swayed by the shocked faces of the assembled detectives, Slater decided to take a chance on this self-styled King of Handcuffs. While it's true that Harry visited Scotland Yard within a week of arriving in town, the rest is probably apocryphal. It's more likely that he gave a series of convincing demonstrations onstage at the Alhambra.

It's certain that a week before opening night there was an afternoon press preview at the Alhambra. Several dozen journalists and detectives watched while Houdini, in formal attire, performed his usual acts, including Metamorphosis, and accepted challenges from members of the press contingent, who had come equipped with various handcuffs and leg irons. Houdini freed himself inside a scarlet tent set up center stage. A committee of spectators invited to inspect the tent voiced skepticism, so the tent was removed and replaced with a shoulder-height, three-paneled screen. Houdini, his hands cuffed behind his back and shackled to leg irons, kneeled awkwardly in front of the screen, facing the audience. The screen obstructed the view of the inspection committee on the stage: they could see that no one was assisting Houdini, but they couldn't see what he was doing with his hands. He shed the restraints one after another, scattering them on the stage floor, unlocked. Suitably impressed, the newspapermen supplied the publicity Slater and Houdini had hoped for.

Booked for a two-week run (which was extended to the end of August), Houdini made his British debut on July 2, 1900, as the tenth act on a bill that included a wide variety of performers, including singers, dancers, and comedians. Featured were a "Boy Juggler," a ventriloquist, a "Fancy Bicyclist," an "Animatograph" (an early motion picture) showing scenes from the front lines of the Boer War, and another illusionist, Chung Ling Soo, an American (real name William Ellsworth Robinson) who had reinvented himself as a "Marvelous Chinese Magician."

The next day the *Evening Standard* reported on a "novel feature in the programme at the Alhambra," the first public appearance in London of "Mr. Harry Houdini": "His dexterity in escaping from handcuffs handed to him by the audience elicited the heartiest applause. Mr. Houdini does not simply slip the shackles from his arms and legs but absolutely unlocks them without the aid of keys or springs. . . . At the conclusion of the severe tests, Mr. Houdini was recalled and applauded again and again." Thunderous curtain calls in a vast, ornate theater. A crowd of thousands roaring its approval. Here at last was the unqualified success he'd always dreamed of.

Except for two quick visits back to the United States to see his family (that is, his mother), Houdini spent the next five years hopping back and forth across the Channel, touring in England and on the continent, mostly Germany, but with forays into many other European countries, with Bess by his side. Everywhere they went, he was received with ovations as gratifying as the ones that had echoed around the Alhambra. His pay skyrocketed: soon he was earning $1,000 per week. He and Bess, he wrote, were just "two young? people roaming around trying to make an honest million." He returned from his first tour of Germany in time for the Christmas season, and a triumphal return engagement at the Alhambra. In the days before the opening night, a dozen men patrolled Leicester Square wearing sandwich boards blazoned with two words "Houdini—Alhambra." He noted in his diary, "Pretty good for Dime Museum Houdini."

Feeling rich, he spoiled his mother. He'd been sending money back to her in New York, but that wasn't enough to show the full measure of his devotion. At the very end of January

1901, as his second run at the Alhambra was coming to a close, he happened to see in the window of a London shop a dress that had been designed for Queen Victoria, who had died just a week or so earlier. He offered to buy it. The shopkeeper hesitated but finally agreed to part with it for £50—on the condition that it never be worn in Great Britain. Years later Harry still remembered his sense of elation: "As I walked out with that dress in my possession, I would not have changed places with any crowned head in the world."

With his eye on his mother's sixtieth birthday (June 17, 1901), he wrote and asked her to join him in Germany, promising a surprise. Cecilia agreed, and caught up with Harry and Bess in Hamburg in April, on the opening night of a month-long run at the Hansa Theater. From Hamburg, they took the train to Budapest, where Harry had decided he would throw a party to show off his mother in royal attire for the delight of the friends and relatives still living in the city twenty-three years after the Weisz family emigrated. He fixed on the Grand Hotel Royal and inquired about holding a reception in the ornate palm garden salon. In a semi-plausible autobiographical fragment found among his papers, he remembered his interview with the hotel manager, who at first refused his request. Harry persisted: "I revealed to him my plot to crown my little mother and allow her to be Queen Victoria for a few fleeting hours. He immediately consented to be my confederate, for the scheme appealed to his sportsmanship, and he said, 'My boy, for so worthy a cause you may have the room for nothing.'" Harry may have made this story up, or greatly exaggerated it (the "sportsmanship" of the Hungarian hotel manager is hard to credit), but the sentiment is surely genuine: Harry wanted his mother to look and feel like a queen.

In his mind, she *was* royalty—he insists on that in his account of the party: "How my heart warmed to see the various friends and relatives kneel and pay homage to my mother, every

inch a queen, as she sat enthroned in her heavily carved and gilded chair."

Having elevated Cecilia to royal rank, he kept her there. Back in New York, she would regularly receive cables from European monarchs, a king or queen sending greetings. The cables were fake, of course, a bit of Houdini magic, but Harry claimed that she "honestly believed it." He may have believed it, too.

* * *

Europe lavished Houdini with praise and filled his pockets with money. He liked England (especially London) and also Germany, where he found the food delicious. He would return again and again on extended tours of England and the continent: from the fall of 1908 until just before the outbreak of the First World War in the summer of 1914, he spent more time abroad than at home. After the war, starting at the very end of 1919, he spent another six months in the United Kingdom.

Yet he never thought of himself as European. On the contrary: being abroad seems to have inspired him to become, officially, more American. Just a few months after first setting foot in England, while still basking in the glow of his instant overseas success, he went to the U.S. embassy on Victoria Street in Westminster and surrendered the passport he'd acquired in May before leaving New York. His aim was to procure a new document that would establish his citizenship beyond all doubt and smooth his path at border crossings on the continent. The passport he surrendered had been that of a naturalized citizen: it marked him as a Hungarian immigrant, his birthplace correctly listed as Budapest. The new passport issued in London declared him a native-born American. He also took the opportunity to grow a couple of inches (he shot up to five foot six) and to change the color of his eyes from brown to blue and his occupation from "actor" to "artiste." The U.S. delegation was apparently willing to overlook these discrepancies and the blatant perjury of an application that contained the phrase "I solemnly swear that I was born at Appleton, in the state of Wisconsin." Houdini's star turn at the Alhambra undoubtedly helped persuade the embassy staff to go along with this bureaucratic fudge. Shouldn't the acclaimed "artiste" (still legally Ehrich

Weiss but "professionally known as 'Harry Houdini, the King of Handcuffs'") carry a passport he could present with absolute confidence, so that he could slip across borders as easily as he shed his cuffs?

Almost as soon as he crossed the English Channel for his first trip to Germany, on September 2, 1900, it became clear that his visit to the U.S. embassy in London had been a smart idea. On the continent, for the first time in his life, he found himself at odds with the civil authorities. Instead of turning up at a police station and offering a demonstration in a friendly spirit, as he did in America, Canada, and England, he received an official summons to appear: all stage performances in the German Empire were subject to censorship, and magic and escapology were no exception. On the contrary, the authorities were keen to prosecute fraud, and conviction could mean heavy fines, imprisonment, or both.

Harry's first stop in Germany was Dresden. It was while performing there, playing to packed houses at the Central Theatre and already booked to appear at the Wintergarten in Berlin, that he was ordered to present himself at police headquarters in the capital. On the afternoon of September 20, he duly appeared at the Polizeipräsidium Alexanderplatz, a vast, imposing edifice known as the Red Castle. Inside, he faced an audience of three hundred officers and assorted representatives of the government of Kaiser Wilhelm II. He was stripped to his underwear and his arms were secured behind his back with an array of devices, including handcuffs, thumbscrews, and finger locks. Leg irons were added for good measure. His mouth was taped shut. Six minutes after a sheet had been thrown over him, he emerged unfettered and deposited his load of iron in a heap on a table. Astonished, the police commissioner, Leopold von Meerscheidt-Hüllessem, decided to endorse Houdini's act rather than censor it. "At this time," the official statement conceded, "we are unable to explain the way in which the locks are opened and remain undamaged."

This was the beginning, not the end, of Houdini's exposure to German law. Nine months later, after wildly successful engagements in Berlin, Hamburg, Frankfurt, Düsseldorf, and Leipzig, he found himself accused of fraud in a Cologne newspaper. In the article, entitled "The Unmasking of Houdini," a policeman accused him of attempted bribery, and a civilian police employee leveled a similar accusation. It was alleged that he tried to fake a jailbreak and cheat during an onstage performance, that he was a charlatan who "swindled" his audience. Leery of any stain on his reputation, and aware that charges such as these could lead to prosecution, Houdini went on the offensive: he hired a lawyer and sued for slander.

The trial, which began on February 19, 1902, and stretched over two long days, ended in a pyrrhic victory for Houdini. Though he won the case (his accusers paid a fine, the newspaper printed a retraction), to clear his name and assure the authorities that his act wasn't fraudulent, he was forced to reveal to the presiding judge his technique for releasing handcuffs. Exposing his secrets was torture. "Just imagine," the *Ausbrecher* confided to a correspondent, "in order to save my honor I had to show how I did it."

In the long run, an adversarial relationship with the authorities worked in his favor. "It does seem strange," he wrote to a friend, "that the people over here, especially Germany, France, Saxony, and Bohemia fear the Police so much, in fact the Police are all Mighty." He recognized, moreover, that this state of affairs presented an opportunity. "I am the first person that has ever dared them," he crowed, "that is my success." He dared them and defeated them, and his name passed into legend.

The brush with the Kaiser's judiciary was just a warm-up for his adventures the following year in Russia, where the regime was more fearsomely autocratic and the presence of the police more pervasive and intrusive. The tour was most likely arranged by a Russian theatrical agent who had seen Houdini's act in Paris, but the details remain mysterious, as does Houdini's motivation. Moscow (where he was booked to perform at the Yar, a venerable restaurant cum music hall) was not a welcoming place for Jews at the turn of the century: more than twenty thousand had been expelled from the city a decade earlier, and strict regulations were in place all over Russia (except in the Pale of Settlement) forbidding the permanent residence of Jews and sometimes excluding them entirely—their mere presence was illegal. Pogroms erupted with dismaying frequency, and 1903, the year of Houdini's visit, was especially violent. A few weeks before he arrived, a horrifying pogrom at Kishinev (now Chişinău, Moldova) killed scores and wounded hundreds, with widespread rape and destruction of property. Houdini performed in Kishinev and saw firsthand traces of the bloody rampage. He had of course been exposed to anti-Semitism before, but not the implacably murderous variety. "I never was ashamed to acknowledge that I was a Jew, and never will be," he'd written to a friend the year before, "but it is awful what I hear from people that are Jew Haters, and do not know that I am a Sheeney."

Houdini seems to have decided to conceal his religion while in Russia. Bess later claimed to have filled out "religious certificates" for both of them; since she was a "Roman Catholic in good standing," they traveled as a Christian couple. Harry was reminded of the risks he would be running before even setting foot in the Russian Empire: at the border their luggage was searched by police who wanted also to rummage through the traveling desk where Harry kept his personal papers—he chose to send it back to Berlin rather than submit to this impromptu audit.

The exotic flavor of faraway Russia, its famous backward-

Chief of the Secret Russian Police LEBEDOEFF has HARRY HOUDINI stripped stark naked and searched then locked up in the Siberian Transport Cell or Carette, May 10/1903 in Moscow and in 28 minutes HOUDINI had made his escape to the unspeakable astonishment of the Russian Police.

HOUDINI in Russia.

ness and brutality, the wealth, the poverty, the omnipotence of the tsar and powerlessness of the serfs, the creeping paranoia of a police state—all this seems to have colored accounts of the five months the Houdinis spent there.

One dubious anecdote about his success at the Yar resembles a surrealist dream sequence. During one of Houdini's performances a Russian army officer resplendent in his uniform planted himself center stage and refused to budge. When the theater manager explained to a baffled and irritated Houdini that the officer considered he had every right as an aristocrat to inconvenience a paid entertainer, Houdini announced that in his country he was known as a "millionaire"—and that magic word compelled the officer to retreat. A suspiciously neat parable about the Old World vanquished by the New.

His legendary escape from the Siberian Transport Cell, a vault on wheels in which unfortunate souls were carted to labor camps in the Russian Far East, is freighted with similarly symbolic overtones. Although the facts are stubbornly hard to establish (did he break out by picking the lock or sawing through the floor or bribing a guard? Did it take him forty-five minutes or twelve?), the meaning of the escape is perfectly clear: Houdini could not be contained by the tsar's dreaded police.

He was unequivocal in asserting that before being thrown into the wagon "in a nude condition," he was subjected to the "severest" search he had ever experienced. Every orifice was probed: "Talk about getting the finger," he wrote to an American friend, "well I received it three times." The police tried and failed to suppress news of the self-liberator's latest feat; word spread that he'd escaped from the Transport Cell, which made him the toast of the town.

He later claimed to have given private performances for the royal family, including Emperor Nicholas II and his uncle Grand Duke Sergei Alexandrovich (who as governor-general of Moscow had overseen the expulsion of the city's Jews), and boasted that he'd been invited to become an advisor to the tsar. Harry and Bess also claimed that it was the grand duke who gave them their beloved pet Charlie, the tiny white Pomeranian that became like a child to them—a royal child, in this telling.

Getting out of Russia seemed another feat of escapology. The red tape at the border was sticky and tangled, as it had been when they arrived, and Harry was thankful "that nothing had happened to transport us to Siberia." He recorded in his diary that he felt the country itself was "some sort of mild prison" from which he was lucky to break free. The things he'd seen, particularly the evidence of assaults on Jews, continued to trouble him. He told a journalist about the "awful state of affairs" in Russia—and that as a result he was "prouder than ever to be an American."

* * *

Europe changed him, and changed his act. He was now an international star—"Europe's Eclipsing Sensation," as the posters proclaimed—and he expected the world to take notice. Touring in Europe was more comfortable than in the U.S.: the engagements longer, the distances shorter, the accommodation more agreeable. He saw Paris and Vienna, Prague and Copenhagen, Amsterdam and Edinburgh. Europe opened his eyes to foreign ways and made him more sophisticated, but it didn't make him calmer or more relaxed. Neither understatement nor the concept of "less is more" ever took hold. Brash, insistent, combative, he remained a man perpetually striving. He still felt the need to exaggerate the fabulousness of each fresh success, trumpeting solid victories so that they sounded more like epic conquests. Most of his time and energy were still devoted to escapology, not only refining and developing his act but also promoting it. Yet at last he had free time and money he could devote to activities not directly related to the advancement of his career.

During his first European tour his habit of poking around in bookshops gradually turned into a compulsion (and in time developed into full-blown bibliomania). Determination and ingenuity—traits essential to his professional life—made him a formidable collector indefatigable in his pursuit of books, pamphlets, playbills, newspaper clippings, and memorabilia. An original program of a performance by an eighteenth- or nineteenth-century conjuror, Pinetti or Bosco or Robert-Houdin, excited him the way a chorus of applause did. At first his interest was limited to the history of magic and the careers of early magicians, but eventually anything involving the theater world became potential quarry. He bought in bulk and shipped his treasures back to New York.

Having decided that he would like to write a kind of biographical encyclopedia of the conjuring arts ("from the time of Moses to the present year"), he became more systematic in his investigations. He began tracking down retired magicians, many of them forgotten old men living in obscurity. He was as dogged in pursuit of these antique gentlemen as he was in his collecting, traveling long distances between shows for a brief interview. Some of the men he chased down had known or even performed with heroes like Robert-Houdin; to talk with them was to approach the mythic sources of modern magic—and also perhaps to revive memories of his father, another old man diminished in his dotage.

He made a habit of visiting the graves of magicians, commissioning photographs of himself at the graveside and even paying for the upkeep of neglected graves. The idea that the final resting place of a once-prominent conjuror should fall into disrepair appalled him.

Early in 1903 he discovered that one of Robert-Houdin's eminent contemporaries, Wiljalba Frikell, was living in seclusion, age eighty-seven, near Dresden. He wrote to him requesting an interview and was rebuffed. He decided to make an unannounced visit and was turned away at the door. He continued to send letters pleading his case, and his persistence paid off: while he was in Russia, he received a note from Frikell saying that the old man would be grateful to accept a packet of a particular brand of Russian tea, which Harry duly sent. Whereupon the longed-for invitation arrived: Professor Frikell would be glad to meet the Great Houdini at the next opportunity. They settled on a date in October, during Houdini's month-long engagement at the Central Theater in Dresden. On the appointed day, he was greeted at Frikell's house by a woman who told him, "You are being waited for." He was led to a room where the old man lay dead, dressed in a suit, his memorabilia arranged around him ready for display. He'd died of a heart attack just two hours earlier. His wife later told Houdini, "If you knew with what yearning my dear dear Frikell had expected you that day." At the funeral, Houdini placed a wreath on the grave on behalf of the Society of American Magicians (SAM).

Houdini had been elected to SAM, which was then in its infancy, early in 1903. During his Russia tour, he began writing monthly reports for *Mahatma*, the society's official publication, a column that appeared under the byline N. Osey. The jocular pseudonym allowed him to take playful jabs at his rivals in the profession. This was his second venture into journalism: in May 1901 he'd begun writing a regular column for a weekly theatrical trade newspaper, the *New York Dramatic Mirror*. The *Dramatic Mirror* column included information on American performers in Europe and tips for those considering tours abroad.

Though he revered retired magicians, and sometimes made friends with magicians who appeared with him on the same bill (such as Chung Ling Soo, the faux-Chinese illusionist he met on his debut at the Alhambra), he was intolerant—sometimes violently intolerant—of competitors he saw as imitators. As a fellow magician remarked, "To anyone who seemed likely to filch a share of his limelight, Houdini was a tyrant." The problem of imitators was aggravated by his European success. "In England we have 55 Kings of Handcuffs," he groused. "If you throw a stone in the air it will fall down and hit some one who has a handcuff key in his pocket and a 'Handcuff King' idea in his head." It was no better on the other side of the Channel: "German performers," he declared, "are, without a doubt, the greatest brain thieves that ever existed."

With habitual bluster and a brash disregard for truth he took out newspaper ads warning his imitators that his handcuff act was "fully patented." (In fact he had abandoned his application for a patent when it became clear that it would entail making public the details of his methods.) He was especially incensed by those imitators who were "using names as near to mine as possible . . . Hourdene, Whodini, Cutini, Stillini, etc." Like other artists and performers who literally made their name with a pseudonym, Harry had strong feelings about his professional moniker. Performers who tried to steal his name posed a profound threat: they were robbing him of his true identity. When in 1913 he finally changed his name legally to Houdini (an application granted by the New York City courts), he was merely making official what had been psychologically and emotionally true for more than a decade: he was Houdini. (Just plain Houdini—Harry seemed to him superfluous.)

In part because of his ubiquitous imitators, he began to emphasize his talents as a jailbreaker—whereupon his imitators did the same. He also worked new tricks into his act, notably the packing crate escape (which he called in private the "nailed up in the box gag"). Introduced in Essen, Germany, in 1902, the packing crate escape was refined a few years later when it became a challenge: local businesses would build boxes for him to break out of. The product placement was a boon for the manufacturer, and Houdini benefited from the naïve trust the audience placed in a crate made by a neighborhood firm. How could there be a gimmick if local craftsmen had built the box? (That's not a rhetorical question. The answer is collusion.)

From the beginning of his career, advertising had been one of Houdini's preoccupations. In Europe he carried on with his municipal jail stunts; his inevitable escape (naked, naturally) from any cell in any city was still a source of excellent free publicity. Having studied with care his copy of Henry Sampson's *History of Advertising from the Earliest Times* (1874), he also began to make aggressive use of print advertising, not just in newspapers and magazines but also flyers and posters that he plastered all over the towns he visited. In 1903 he issued his first "pitch book," a twelve-page pamphlet boasting immoderately of the accomplishments of *America's Sensational Perplexer*. In it he claimed to have "broke[n] more records for drawing paid Admissions than any other act in the annals of Show History." Sold cheaply or handed out for free by the tens of thousands, the pamphlet was the first of many he produced and distributed over the years, each successive version an exercise in stretching superlatives to their utmost. As in all things, he insisted on beating the competition; he declared himself satisfied that he was "the best advertised man that ever crossed the vaudeville stage in Europe." A prominent fellow magician, T. Nelson Downs ("King of Koins"), impressed by all this tireless and ingenious self-promotion, astutely labeled him "the P. T. Barnum of today."

He cooked up one of his most amusing promotions for his premiere at the Paris Olympia in late November 1901. He hired seven bald men and had one letter of his name painted on each hairless head. These gentlemen would sit in a row at a café on a crowded boulevard, bow reverentially, and remove their hats in sequence so that H-O-U-D-I-N-I was spelled out by their bald pates.

This first visit to Paris lasted two and a half months. Harry and Bess rented an apartment—"a little home of our own"—at 32 rue Bellefond in the 9th arrondissement, about a ten-minute walk from the Place Pigalle. They were joined there for the holidays by Harry's younger brother Dash. For the last year or so Dash had been performing as Hardeen—Houdini's only sanctioned imitator. Harry was at once loyal to Dash and competitive with him. He was happy to have Hardeen be the lesser of the two escape artists in the family, especially if the mock rivalry generated publicity.

In January he traveled a hundred-odd miles southwest of Paris to the Loire Valley town of Blois, birthplace of Robert-Houdin and also the site of his grave. Harry had written to Robert-Houdin's widowed daughter-in-law asking permission to pay her a visit and to lay a wreath on the grave. She refused on both counts. Undeterred, he embarked on the four-hour train ride. As a memento of the journey, he mailed to himself a postcard of Blois (of a banal street in the town rather than the famous chateau) with the date, "Jan 28/1902," carefully noted. Back in Paris, on stationery from the town's Grand Hotel, he typed (or mistyped), "Hotel I stoped at during my visit to Blois France, visiting the grave of Robert-Houdin." He was generating his very own memorabilia.

* * *

In the spring of 1903, just before the trip to Russia, in a sign of his increasing prosperity (and of his new dependence on bulky apparatus), he hired his first full-time assistant, the Austrian-born Franz Kukol. Like every subsequent assistant, Kukol was required to sign an oath pledging never to divulge the secrets of Houdini's act. Kukol's job called for many diverse talents: he had to perform onstage, taking up all Bess's duties except Metamorphosis; see to the printing and distribution of promotional material; act as Houdini's personal photographer; and organize transport for the Houdini household, including the dog, the ever-expanding library, the professional equipment, and the personal belongings—in all as many as a half dozen steamer trunks, plus a half dozen more chests, hampers, and cases.

There's some doubt about the length of Kukol's service. On March 2, 1913, exactly ten years after hiring him, Houdini interrupted his performance at the Empire Theatre in Finsbury Park, London, and presented to his faithful assistant a gold pocket watch and chain to commemorate their decade together. It's likely that the association ended four years later when the U.S. declared war on Germany, and Kukol returned to Europe. (His wife and children, including a son named Harry Houdini Kukol, lived in Austria.) But there's also evidence to suggest that Kukol was still in America and still in Houdini's employ as late as 1924. Either way, it was a long and harmonious partnership founded on the employee's enduring loyalty and discretion, the two qualities Harry most prized in his assistants.

Kukol couldn't help with the challenges Houdini faced alone onstage, behind the curtain of his cabinet, as he struggled with a restraint brought to him by a member of the public eager to collect the promised cash prize for baffling the American self-liberator. Perhaps the single most dramatic challenge came in March 1904, when a reporter from the *London Daily Illustrated Mirror* climbed onto the stage of the Hippodrome and dared Houdini to free himself from a pair of cuffs made by a master blacksmith from Birmingham who claimed to have spent five years manufacturing them and insisted that the lock could not be picked by "mortal man." Houdini refused, arguing that the homemade cuffs were not "regulation." Goaded by the reporter, Houdini accepted the challenge—with a show of reluctance, as though the possibility of defeat were real. A date was set and a massive publicity campaign unleashed by the *Mirror* and the Hippodrome. It worked: four thousand people bought tickets for the matinee on Thursday, March 17; as many as a hundred journalists flocked to the theater to cover the story.

This carefully orchestrated contest featured moments of brilliant Houdini showmanship. At three o'clock, after a half dozen warm-up acts had entertained the swelling crowd, Houdini strode onto the stage and announced grandly, "I am ready to be manacled by the *Mirror* representative if he be present." Having been duly handcuffed by the reporter, who turned the key six times to drive the bolt home, the escape artist slipped behind his screen. The orchestra played, the audience waited. After twenty-two minutes, Houdini poked his head out and was greeted by enthusiastic cheers—but it turned out he only wanted to get a look at the lock in better light. The band struck up a waltz. After thirty-five minutes, he again emerged, this time looking hot and bothered and complaining that his knees hurt. Might he have a cushion? The request was approved, a cushion produced. The Mysteriarch retreated behind the screen and the wait went on. After fifty-five minutes, he reappeared, still manacled and seemingly exhausted. He appeared to be drenched in sweat. "Would you remove the handcuffs for a moment," he asked his challenger, "in order that I may take my coat off?" This request was refused: "I cannot unlock those cuffs," the journalist replied, "unless you admit you are defeated." Houdini then astonished and delighted his audience by extracting a penknife from his waistcoat pocket, opening it with his teeth, holding it in his mouth, flipping his coat over his head, and slashing the garment to pieces. The crowd roared its approval. Houdini retreated again—by now he had been cuffed for a full hour. Ten minutes later, as the band played a rousing march, Houdini bounced out from behind the screen, holding the cuffs aloft in one hand. He was free, the crowd jubilant. Hoisted on shoulders, he was paraded around the stage. The *Mirror* reported that Houdini sobbed during these celebrations: "the strain had been too much for the 'Handcuff King.'"

The details of the performance were reported in newspapers all over the country. To whip up still more excitement, Houdini published a dare aimed at his rivals and imitators: "I hereby challenge any mortal being to open the MIRROR Handcuff in the same space of time that I did. I will allow him the full use of both hands; also any instrument or instruments, barring the actual key. The cuff must not be broken or spoilt. Should he succeed I will forfeit 100 guineas." The Hippodrome doubled down on its advertising blitz. Harry wrote to an American correspondent, "Talk about being billed big, you ought to see London, and look about. Nothing on the walls but Houdini."

In early summer 1904, just before leaving England for a three-month vacation in the U.S., Harry bought a Humber motorcar and had it shipped across the Atlantic, a hint that his time in Europe was drawing to a close. Surprisingly, he was not a good driver. Although mechanically minded and supremely dexterous, he couldn't seem to sustain concentration when behind the wheel. The essential business of steering the vehicle made him simultaneously anxious and bored. He preferred to be driven—but he was a nervous passenger. This might be a rare instance of his courage failing him, or it might be a question of risk astutely assessed: automobile accidents, at the turn of the century, were terrifyingly common.

The European adventures that made Houdini famous and

rich enough to spend his money on a dangerous novelty such as an automobile also persuaded him that he wanted to settle down. During his summer visit to America he bought not one but two houses: a large brownstone in Harlem (for which he paid $25,000) and a sixty-eight-acre farm near Stamford, Connecticut. He also bought a family burial plot in a Jewish cemetery in Queens, to which he promptly transferred the remains of his father, his maternal grandmother, and his half brother, Herman. A final resting place for the peripatetic Harry.

Life on tour was exciting and also wearying, even for a person as tenacious and resilient as Harry. To perform day after day, night after night, is emotionally taxing—and bruising, too, for the body. But before he could give himself a rest—in town, on the farm, or in the grave—he had obligations to meet, performances scheduled all over England, in Scotland and Wales, and also in Paris. Not until a year later, in the summer of 1905, would he get a chance to cross the Atlantic again and enjoy his new properties.

Harry was back in Great Britain and had just celebrated his thirty-first birthday when a controversy that had simmered for some months boiled over, and a messy, violent scene ensued. The incident brought together many of the frustrating aspects of his nomadic existence, including troublesome rivals and high-handed, litigious theater owners.

The theater owner in this instance was Horace Edward Moss, whose extensive chain of vaudeville theaters included the London Hippodrome. Moss had hired Houdini in 1902 for a twenty-week period at £100 per week, and retained an option to book him for a further twenty weeks at the same rate. In the beginning of 1904, Moss tried to exercise that option, but Harry, who was now making £125 a week, refused. Moss sued and lost, sued again and lost again. Then he hired a Houdini imitator called Frank Hilbert to shadow Houdini, playing in Moss circuit theaters in whatever town Houdini was playing. Hilbert's show was called "The Burst Bubble—How Handcuff Tricks Are Done."

Houdini was unamused. "The very managers that I have made thousands of pounds for," he complained, "are now trying to ruin the act for England." On April 10, 1905, the day he was opening at the King's Theatre in the gritty coal port of Cardiff, and Hilbert was opening at the Cardiff Empire, a Moss-owned theater, Houdini took matters into his own hands. As it happened, his brother Dash (aka Hardeen) and their younger sister Gladys were traveling with him and Bess. They all bought tickets to Hilbert's show—even Harry, who was in disguise. He knew that the Moss organization had warned the manager of the Empire not to admit him to any performance, and "to eject him should he attempt to create disorder." In the afternoon before the show, Houdini had been to a hairdresser to have his hair dyed gray; he'd fashioned for himself a fake nose made of wax, and acquired spectacles, a false moustache, and a cane—so when he turned up at the box office of the Empire he was an old man who looked nothing like Harry Houdini.

Create disorder is exactly what he did, abetted by his loyal family. When Hilbert was in the midst of his act, Houdini yelled out, projecting with the force of a seasoned performer, "You're a fraud, you're a damned fraud." His wife and sister stood up and they too started shouting and waving about a pair of regulation handcuffs, which they insisted Hilbert would be unable to open. The theater manager had taken the precaution of requesting a police presence for the performance, and Houdini, who was waving his cane and yelling abuse at Hilbert, soon found that two constables were offering to escort him from the hall. Houdini resisted, and later claimed that that the manager grabbed him by the throat and shoved him at the constables, one of whom kneed him in the ribs. Dash tried to come to his rescue, to no avail—but loudly warned Hilbert that he would be back to disrupt every performance. The constables eventually threw Houdini out a side door of the Empire, down four steps into a muddy alley. He landed on his back. According to Houdini, when he got up, fearing that his leg was broken, and tried to walk away, the theater manager gave him a kick.

Houdini insisted on pressing assault charges against the manager, but the Cardiff magistrates' court dismissed the case. What he wrote in his diary about the tussle with Hilbert and company suggests he was nonetheless satisfied with the outcome: "Went disguised, was carried out. Raised hell in the streets. This helped my business. Papers full of account." The "rumpus" boosted ticket sales for the remainder of his run at the King's Theatre. A shabby episode—yet as usual Houdini wanted the last laugh.

4

———◆◄◆►◆———

Return of the Hero

HAVING MADE HIS NAME in Europe in spectacular fashion, Houdini was determined to do better still in America—as though he had challenged himself to surpass his foreign feats on home turf.

First he took a break, spending the second half of the summer of 1905 on his recently acquired farm in Connecticut. Not surprisingly, Harry's idea of leisure time involved strenuous physical tasks (such as felling trees, clearing boulders for a driveway, and building stone steps to a henhouse) as well as self-promotion. He took time in mid-August to visit the offices of the local newspaper, the *Stamford Advocate*, where he charmed a local journalist: "Personally, Houdini is one of the most agreeable men to meet, is modest and unassuming and has not the usual manners of the stage performer . . . his cosmopolitan experience has given him an air of assurance."

Having explained with cosmopolitan self-assurance his plans

for improving the farm, and having confided to the reporter how pleased he was to have found a quiet spot where he could rest and his mother could enjoy bucolic surroundings, he promptly put the property up for sale. Just weeks after the interview, he placed an ad in the *Advocate* asking $7,500 for what he claimed with characteristic hyperbole was "positively the healthiest place on a hill this side of Denver." The farm was sold in October, barely thirteen months after he'd purchased it. Country life didn't suit the Houdinis after all.

In truth, the whole concept of rest was alien to him. As he told his lawyer in the last year of his life, "You know five hours is a full night's sleep for me. I can do with less. . . . Maybe that's one of the reasons I am the Great Houdini instead of a side-show piker." His return to America and his plan to conquer the New World as he had conquered the Old coincided with the first rumblings about retiring from show business altogether, an unconvincing refrain he sounded every few years over the next two decades. The implausible notion of Houdini in retirement—picture him dozing in a hammock—may have been something he trotted out for the press with half an eye on ticket sales for his next tour: *Last Chance to See the Great Houdini!*

Home, for this fundamentally restless man, was now the big Harlem brownstone, 278 West 113th Street. With more than a dozen rooms on four floors, over the next twenty years it housed various members of his extended family, among them his mother, mother-in-law, older brother Bill (the only serious drinker in the Weiss family), sister Gladys, and youngest brother Leo, who had graduated from medical school in 1899 with a specialty in a brand new branch of medicine now known as radiology. Leo set up an office at 278 (as the house was known in the family), and installed an X-ray machine. Harry himself was in residence only infrequently, but that didn't keep him from expressing his pride in what he called "the finest private house that any magician has ever had the great fortune to possess."

This part of Harlem, a few blocks from the northern end of Central Park and a ten-minute stroll across Morningside Park from Columbia University, was a prime destination for Jews who had earned enough to escape tenements in more crowded areas of the city. Harry's house was a suitably solid-looking structure, with rusticated stonework on the lower portion of the façade. Inside, there was enough wood paneling to make it seem grand, though somewhat dark on the first two floors. Even when it was only notionally his home, the house provided continuity. A fixed point for a man perpetually on the road, it served as a library for his rapidly expanding collection of books about magic and theater, a museum for his mementos, and a laboratory for developing new tricks and escapes.

An extra-large bathtub he had installed in 278 was particularly useful when working on underwater effects—which in the fall of 1905 were much on his mind. Before his American tour opened in New York with a two-week run at the Colonial Music Hall, a newly constructed theater on Broadway and 62nd Street big enough to hold an audience of thirteen hundred, he cooked up a promotional stunt that was recorded in detail in several local newspapers, including the *New York Times*. The *Times* article, "A Shackle-Breaking Match under Water," which appeared on September 21, 1905, is a colorful account of the "performance" staged the day before, a contest between Houdini and a character who called himself Jacques Boudini (whose name the *Times* misspells throughout as "Bondini"):

> Harry Houdini, the "sensational perplexer and mysteriarch," professional shackle and handcuff breaker, had made a wager with Jacques Bondini that he could break manacles from his hands and ankles quicker than he. Houdini has been abroad startling Kings with his performances of handcuff breaking and making them wonder what to do next with their criminals. When recently Houdini returned to this country he found that Bondini, his erstwhile pupil, was usurping his field

here. That's the story as the press agent tells it. At all events Houdini challenged Bondini to a shackle-breaking match under water. The victor was to get $500.

There's no evidence that Boudini was ever Houdini's pupil or that he threatened to usurp Houdini's place; in fact, this cameo appearance in the annals of escapology is his only claim to fame. The *Times* reporter's pointed reference to the press agent's "story" makes it clear from the beginning that the challenge was a publicity scam: Boudini was Houdini's creation. But the "challenge" was Houdini's first public attempt at underwater shackle-breaking, providing an entertaining spectacle for the assembled journalists and offering a window on Houdini's unending efforts to hone his showmanship.

Houdini, Boudini, and a band of reporters were ferried by tug boat to the middle of the Atlantic Basin, a sheltered body of water surrounded by Brooklyn piers and shipbuilding yards, where the two contestants stripped down to their trunks for the ordeal. They were shackled with hand and ankle cuffs, ropes were fastened around their waists, and they were lowered into the water. The *Times* journalist enjoyed a ringside seat:

There was a silence as thick as a fog. . . . It lasted one minute and thirty seconds, but that seemed an eternity to the watchers. Then a head appeared above the waves. It was that of Houdini. He spat out brine for a second and shouted:

"Is Bondini up yet?"

"No!" chorused the crowd on deck.

Houdini stuck his hands above water to show that he had freed them of the shackles and disappeared again.

A minute later the head of Bondini appeared above the water. He looked gloomy, and it was obvious that he was not having any luck. He was down again in a minute.

In another minute and ten seconds the head of Houdini appeared.

"Is Bondini up yet?" he asked.

The answer was discouraging, so far as Bondini was concerned, but encouraging for Houdini. Houdini went down a third time, but not until he had stuck one foot above water to show that he had unfastened his ankle bracelets, too.

The contest was over. "More dead than alive," the hapless Boudini was hauled up onto the tug by the rope around his midriff, manacles still locked on wrists and ankles. Victory belonged to Houdini—but the jaded *Times* reporter was not convinced that the $500 prize would ever be paid:

> The question which the skeptical were asking last night was:
> "Was Bondini merely a dummy intended to show off the skill of Houdini?"
> Nobody answered except the press agent.
> "The real thing," said he.

If newspaper coverage was the aim of the exercise, the outing was a success, though the skepticism of the reporter suggests that Houdini had yet to perfect underwater escapology.

A little over a year later, he found the twist that would make this kind of escape compelling: instead of allowing himself to be lowered into the water with a rope, he jumped. On November 27, 1906, he stood manacled on the railing of the Belle Isle Bridge in Detroit and plunged twenty-five feet into the icy current of the Detroit River, a "remarkable feat"—or in any case applauded as such on the front page of the *Detroit News*. For nearly a decade bridge jumps became his signature publicity stunt, drawing huge crowds and generating reams of press coverage. If he visited a city, he would announce his arrival either by breaking out of the municipal jail or by jumping from a landmark bridge—or both.

He wasn't the first performer to jump off a bridge, or even the first to leap into the water manacled—that honor belongs to a British magician who jumped handcuffed into the North Sea from a pier in Great Yarmouth in 1901. Six years earlier, Robert

Emmet Odlum had leapt from the recently built Brooklyn Bridge, hoping the feat would secure him fame and fortune; he died in the attempt. A dubious character named Steve Brodie claimed to have survived a jump from the Brooklyn Bridge, but probably faked it. Inspired by Brodie, Larry Donovan tried to make a name for himself as "the champion aerial jumper of the world" by hurling himself off a succession of high bridges, including the Brooklyn Bridge. He achieved a minor celebrity, but riches eluded him. After crossing the Atlantic in 1888 in search of fresh challenges, the unlucky Donovan drowned in the Thames after leaping from a railroad bridge on a £2 bet. The obituary in the *New York Sun* quoted his mother: "I told him that jumping off bridges was a poor way of earning a living."

Film footage of Houdini's jump in Rochester, New York, from the Weighlock Bridge into the Erie Canal on May 7, 1907 (the earliest motion picture of Houdini in action), illustrates the utter simplicity and wild popularity of the stunt. A cameraman on the bridge picks out Houdini as he stands among a dozen gentlemen bundled in coats—it's clearly a chilly day, more like March than May. Some of the men could be reporters, some civil authorities. There are two uniformed policemen. Everyone except Houdini is wearing a hat or a cap, but that's not the only difference: Houdini is the sole object of attention, every eye on him as he rapidly strips off coat, jacket and vest, necktie, suspenders, shirt, shoes and socks, and finally trousers, all dropped in a heap beside him. When he's peeled off everything except white trunks that come down nearly to his knees, one of the policemen fastens two pairs of cuffs on his wrists. The other policeman checks that they're secure.

Houdini raises his manacled arms above his head for all to see, then starts to clamber up onto the bridge truss, at which point the film's perspective changes: we follow the action from the towpath of the canal. We see a small man in white trunks climbing up, finding his balance, then standing tall on the truss.

He adjusts the manacles on his wrists, stretches out his arms, brings them down in front of him, as though he were making an offering. Beyond the bridge, on the other side of the canal, we glimpse a portion of the crowd; they're jammed into every available space. (According to the *Rochester Union and Advertiser*, ten thousand people are watching, and those in prime spots have been there, eager for the action, for two hours.) Intrepid spectators cling to the iron girders of the bridge, just yards away from Houdini—but he's all alone up there, building suspense merely by waiting. Then he leaps, spreading his legs briefly—a flourish—before splashing explosively into the water. The drop is some fifty feet, yet he surfaces within seconds, brandishing the open cuffs above his head before swimming to the towpath to be welcomed by the cheering throng.

The film is silent, of course, but the newspaper reports that he yelled "Good-bye" before jumping, a neat bit of showmanship. It's clearly a hazardous stunt, and he did everything he could think of to dramatize the risk. "The easiest way to attract a crowd," he once wrote, "is to let it be known that at a given time and a given place someone is going to attempt something that in the event of failure will mean sudden death." He kept in his diary an item clipped from the *London Daily Mail* about a "so-called Handcuff King" who died on April 16, 1909, after jumping manacled from a bridge: "He failed in the attempt and was drowned." Harry scribbled a postscript—"Failure meant a lingering death"—suggesting that he had fully imagined the specific kind of doom he was courting.

The threat of death, lingering or sudden, helps explain the size and enthusiasm of the crowd: they were there to see him succeed—or fail. What's most striking about the film of the Rochester jump is the isolation of the hero. The spectators form an indistinguishable mass, a faceless mob. Houdini, in his white trunks, with heavy irons on his wrists, is poignantly alone, a solitary figure bravely facing mortal danger.

* * *

He was courting death, and courting immortality, too—not just through his performances but also through his literary endeavors. He had come to believe that reading and writing were a crucial part of his heritage. He claimed to have "records for five generations that my direct fore-fathers were students and teachers of the Bible and recognized as among the leading bibliographers of their times." In 1906, Houdini took his place in this long line of bibliographers (did he mean *bibliophiles? Bibliolaters?*) by publishing his first book, *The Right Way to Do Wrong*; launching a magazine, *Conjuror's Monthly*; and beginning research for *The Unmasking of Robert-Houdin*, which he finished writing in July 1907 and published in May of the following year.

A brief, breezy book about the tricks of the criminal trade, *The Right Way to Do Wrong* was almost certainly not written by Houdini himself. The slick, easy tone bears no relation to the way he expressed himself in his diary or his correspondence. He provided the raw material (he knew plenty of police officers and shady characters and liked hearing and telling stories about criminality)—but the prose style came from elsewhere. Consider, for example, the particularly ungenerous chapter "Beggars and Deadbeats" in which we're told, "Beggars there have been since civilization created the distinctions of wealth and poverty and must needs be till a higher, better civilization makes misery and crime impossible or unnecessary. For ages the mendicant has flourished, plying his vocation on the credulous and making profit out of the fact that humanity and religion make almsgiving a virtue." Sounds more like a hired hack (possibly his press agent, Whitman Osgood) than a frantically busy escape artist with no formal education.

The twenty-three issues of *Conjuror's Monthly Magazine*, which lasted just under two years, were by contrast very Houdini-like in both tone and content, though his prose was again polished by hired helpers. A trade magazine with a highly personal slant (one rival magazine editor remarked with some justification that the periodical was "intended primarily as an advertisement for the owner"), it was full of show business gossip and score-settling and log-rolling—as well as useful news. It was copiously illustrated with items from Houdini's growing collection of handbills and posters. His written contributions, especially in the section entitled "Reading and Rubbish: Reviewing Books and Things from the Press, Wise and Otherwise," were intemperate, to say the least. A random sample, from a review of a book on spirit mediums: "After careful perusal of the contents, without any fear of contradiction, we can say that of all the books on this subject of which we have ever heard or read, this reaches the pinnacle of absolute imbecilic rot." Elsewhere his venom was concentrated, as usual, on imitators and rivals; he used the magazine as a club to batter them.

In the first year of *Conjuror's Monthly*, Houdini published a dozen installments of what would eventually become *The Unmasking of Robert-Houdin*. From the beginning he made it clear that he was planning a reappraisal, thirty-five years after the Frenchman's death, of Robert-Houdin's "proper place" in the history of magic. The finished book was something more fierce and bizarre: it amounted to literary patricide. The conjuror whose memoirs had fired the young Ehrie Weiss with a passion for magic and launched him in his profession, the man whose namesake he became—his "guide and hero," he had called him—was now deemed a charlatan, "a mere pretender," a "Prince of Pilferers." A "day of reckoning" was at hand: Houdini declared Robert-Houdin "uncrowned."

The Unmasking marks a crucial moment in Houdini's life. With this appalling jumble of a book, part brutal diatribe, part patchwork history of magic, the author sought to elevate himself above the fray, to proclaim himself unrivaled. (As he memorably put it when assessing his dexterity as a manipulator of playing cards, "With due modesty, I can say that I recognize no one as my peer.") He felt the same way about his book, distributing at performances handbills that challenged the reading public to find "in all the literature of magic, one book that can compare with mine."

The vehemence of the attack on Robert-Houdin was matched by its blindness. Houdini condemned his erstwhile hero's "supreme egotism and utter disregard for the truth"; accused him of stealing tricks from other magicians and "an utter unwillingness to admit any ability in his rivals"; derided his talent as a conjuror; and denounced him for using a ghostwriter. All these charges were repeatedly and plausibly leveled at Houdini himself, then and now—yet at no point did he see the irony in his furious denunciations. As Gertrude Stein once remarked, "There is nothing we are more intolerant of than our own sins writ large in others."

In the days when Freudian theory was widely and eagerly embraced, it would have been easy to fix a label on Harry's troubling behavior, to gesture meaningfully toward his intense devotion to his mother and call his patricidal attack on Robert-Houdin symptomatic of an unresolved Oedipus complex. (One biographer did just that.) But labeling and understanding are two different things, and some doubt lingers about his conscious and unconscious motives. Adam Phillips has pointed out, "The masked are always great unmaskers." In this instance, Houdini was barely masked at all: his raw ambition and relentless drive were openly displayed. He may have been oblivious to the embarrassing ugliness of what he was doing not because it was unconscious but because his eyes were firmly fixed on posterity. The attempt to assassinate his hero was meant to take the competition with rivals to a higher plane: no longer focused on ticket sales for next week's show, he was thinking about the sweep of history and posterity's judgment. It was deathless fame he was after, a place in the pantheon—where there clearly wasn't room for both Houdini and Robert-Houdin.

The book was poorly received, and Robert-Houdin's reputation survived the assault; he's still today known as the Father of Modern Magic. But 1908 marks the end of his role as Houdini's progenitor—from then on the escapologist was doubly fatherless. *The Unmasking* is dedicated to the memory of "Rev. M. S. Weiss, Ph.D., LL.D., who instilled in me love of study and patience in research"—yet the tribute to his biological father (here burdened with an unsuitable honorific and university degrees he never earned) can't disguise the fact that Houdini now thought of himself as self-made: a self-generated self-liberator.

In fact, he generated not one escape artist but two: himself and his brother. He had urged Dash to take up escapology and even chose the name Hardeen for him, with the idea that fierce competition with a younger brother would make for good publicity. But as always with Houdini, the situation was emotionally complicated; genuine sibling rivalry was mixed with faux rivalry and made the relationship rocky at times.

Like his brother, Hardeen found his first sustained success in Europe. He spent a half dozen years on tour, forging his reputation as a first-class Houdini imitator. In the summer of 1907 he was ready to come home, and Houdini helped arrange a U.S. tour on a competing vaudeville circuit—and then set about planting stories in the press about fraternal rivalry. When a report about the return of Hardeen cropped up in a New York newspaper, it alluded to Houdini's suspicion that his brother "was coming from Europe to drive him from the stage." On August 16, when the RMS *Teutonic* sailed into New York harbor, Houdini, along with a crowd of reporters, was there to meet him; he hitched a ride on a revenue cutter and boarded the White Star steamship before it reached the docks. Watched by the press, the two brothers parleyed at length on the deck of the *Teutonic*, after which they made themselves available for interviews. Having explained that he had come to greet his brother and "learn his intentions"—because he'd been "very much alarmed" by his return—Houdini reassured the reporters that a rift between the siblings had been averted: "He says that he will not antagonize me . . . and will not attempt to discredit my name of 'Houdini,' though he is under contract to work in this country. We have always loved each other, and I felt very badly when I heard he was going to fight me, but I guess the country is big enough for both of us."

As usual, Houdini's play for publicity worked exactly as intended, and the two brothers kept at it for the next decade. The trouble was that Houdini insisted on winning every round of this sham wrestling match. When a crack Hardeen made about admiring his brother so much that he'd be willing to hire him as an assistant made its way into print, the older sibling was not amused. "It got Harry on my neck," Dash remembered, "and there was nothing synthetic about his anger." Harry told him he'd gone too far; Dash promised not to make the same mistake again—"and good feeling was restored."

* * *

For his conquest of America Houdini relied more and more on death-defying stunts. To capture onstage the razor-edge thrill of the bridge jumps, he turned to tricks that looked to the audience like punishment or torture, some potentially fatal, others merely grueling. He was strapped into a straitjacket and in plain sight of the spectators—no cabinet, no curtain—wriggled and writhed and thrashed his way free, emerging exhausted, sweaty, abraded. He added a perilous twist to the packing crate escapes: he was stuffed, manacled, into airtight containers filled with water, which entailed a race against the clock—he had to break out before he drowned. And then came the Water Torture Cell (which he called USD for upside down), which made his apparently hopeless predicament visible to all: the audience watched as he was lowered headfirst into the water; they could see him there through the glass, underwater, clearly doomed. The wits on the vaudeville circuit dubbed Houdini's act the "Death and Resurrection Show."

After introducing his first escape from a water-filled container in early 1908, he found he had no suitable name for it. He offered a $25 reward for a bright idea, but none materialized. The prosaic name it goes by today derives from the shape of the container: the Milk Can escape.

Showmanship and the threat of mortal danger made the trick compelling. Houdini and his assistants presented the galvanized iron can onstage. He boasted of its sturdy construction. The usual committee of volunteers came up to inspect and verify. Then Houdini went into the wings to change into his bathing trunks while Kukol and the other assistants filled the can with twenty-odd pails of water. When Houdini returned, he asked the audience members to participate in a trial run of sorts: they were to hold their breath while he submerged himself in the can. He stepped in and shimmied down so that only his head protruded over the rim, displaced water sloshing over the sides. The assistants topped it up. He took a deep breath—along with the entire audience—and sank out of sight. As the seconds ticked by, the spectators felt the strain, their lungs beginning to ache, and one by one they gave up, exhaling gratefully. Many more seconds passed before Houdini popped up again. And now for the real thing. Handcuffs were fastened to his wrists and he lowered himself into the water, which was again topped up. Six padlocks secured the lid to the top of the can. A cabinet was brought forward, its curtain drawn to hide the can. The orchestra struck up "Asleep in the Deep." Kukol brandished his ax—just in case Houdini failed to emerge. But after two minutes, or even three—an eternity for the waiting crowd—he suddenly appeared, sweeping open the curtain to

reveal the can, still padlocked. He himself was dripping wet and drawing ragged breaths. Wild cheers from the astounded audience.

"The new Can trick is the best that I have ever invented," he bragged in a letter. "It's a fine-looking trick, and almost defies detection." (He had offered Bess $10 if she could guess how it was done; "She failed to fathom the trick," he wrote in his diary. "GOOD.") And yet he worked on improvements. He designed what he claimed was the world's largest stopwatch: the movement of the second hand allowed the audience to measure the marvel of his underwater endurance tick by tick. He substituted other liquids for water: milk from local cows, beer from local breweries. He had the can placed in a mammoth wooden chest, banded with steel, and padlocked. He tried unsuccessfully to figure out how to nest the can upside down inside another, larger can, also filled with water.

The ultimate improvement to the Milk Can was the Chinese Water Torture Cell, for which he had the idea as early as 1909. He had the cell built in England under the supervision of an assistant named Jim Collins, at a reported cost of more than $10,000. Houdini was in England for the first six months of 1911; in March he was still consulting about details of the cell's design. The next month, at the Hippodrome Theatre in Southampton, he staged the one and only performance of a brief drama entitled *Challenged; or, Houdini Upside Down*, the sole purpose of which was to copyright the act as a play. Houdini made it known far and wide that he had obtained "special license" from the lord chamberlain, and that he was prepared to take legal action to deter imitators: "I will certainly stop anyone infringing on my rights."

The public debut of the Water Torture Cell came a year and a half later, on September 21, 1912, at Circus Busch, Berlin. The gleaming apparatus, made of polished Honduran mahogany, nickel-plated steel, and tempered glass, stood on a tarpaulin spread across the stage. It reeked of menace. Brass handles, brass hasps, brass padlocks stood out against the nickel. The assistants, in brocaded uniforms—which they later covered with shiny black foul-weather gear—looked like acolytes taking part in some sinister sacrifice. The cruel stocks added to the impression, as did the waiting ax. The winching up of the victim, the heart-stopping pause before he was lowered headfirst into

the water, the sight of him jammed upside down in that glass coffin—*torture* was the right word. The curtain closed, the ex-cruciating wait began. At the exact moment when the entire audience had become convinced that catastrophe had struck, out he popped, gasping, eyes bloodshot, lips flecked with foam. It was indeed a resurrection.

Audiences roared their approval, and the critics concurred. Houdini wrote to a fellow magician that this was "without doubt the greatest spectacular thing ever witnessed on the stage." He thought of it as "the climax of all my studies and labors." He performed the escape hundreds of times, in dozens of cities; on his last tour, at the age of fifty-two, he was still inflicting this special brand of torture on himself.

Despite all his precautions, an imitator—Miss Undina— appeared just months after the Berlin debut. Houdini obtained an injunction to halt her performances. He then decided that he might as well manage the competition. He hired a woman named Wanda Timm, provided her with a cell like his own, coached her performance, and rechristened her Miss Trixy. She was, of course, sworn to secrecy. Houdini's anointed surrogate, she toured the continent, doing especially well in Germany and Russia.

On January 6, 1913, at the Cardiff Empire—the same Moss Brothers theater where a disguised Houdini had caused a "rumpus" eight years earlier—he gave the first public performance in Great Britain of the Water Torture Cell. The American debut came six months later, at Hammerstein's Roof Garden in what is now Times Square, less than a week after his return from Europe.

The advent of the Water Torture Cell coincided with the end of his jailbreaks. These had become elaborate affairs, often involving the cells of notorious criminals. In January 1906, on his very first visit to the nation's capital, Houdini broke out of the cell in the United States Jail that had once held Charles Guiteau, the assassin who shot President James Garfield in 1881. Guiteau received death threats while he was imprisoned, and the authorities, concerned lest a vigilante murder their inmate before the state had a chance to execute him, had put a bulletproof oak door on his cell. Not content with merely escaping from behind the assassin's customized door, Houdini took the opportunity to rehouse all the inmates on death row, shuffling them into new cells. Impressed rather than offended, the warden provided Houdini with a fulsome certificate explaining that there was "positively no chance for any confederacy or collusion."

Two months later, in Boston, the superintendent of police locked Houdini's clothes into cell no. 77 on the ground floor of the Somerset Street jail and Houdini himself, limbs encumbered with the usual handcuffs and leg irons, into cell no. 60 on the second floor. Sixteen minutes later, the self-liberator was scaling the prison wall fully dressed and scampering up the street in the direction of Keith's Theater, where he was performing that evening.

The next month found him in Salem, Massachusetts. "Stark naked" (except for three pairs of handcuffs and two pairs of leg irons), Houdini was locked in one cell of the police station, his clothes in another. After releasing himself and his clothing, dressing himself, and handcuffing himself to a prisoner he released from a third cell, he slipped out of the jailhouse, ran around the building to find the window of the office where the city marshal and other officials had just settled in to wait, and waved hello.

The drill was the same or similar all over America and Europe, in cities large and small. Then, in the spring of 1912, he suddenly gave it up. It may have been because there was no danger involved, and no crowds to speak of—only the warden, the guards, and the inmates. Or it may have been that he was simply running out of prisons. Virtually every penitentiary of note had already "hosted" a Houdini jailbreak, or refused to let him try.

The other pillar of his promotional routine—jumping, manacled, from bridges, piers, and every variety of boat into rivers, bays, and basins—continued uninterrupted. In the two years after cameramen had immortalized on film the jump in Roch-

PHOTO BY
WALTER J. BERRY.
-BOSTON GLOBE-

ester, Houdini did it again, more than a dozen times, on either side of the continent and the other side of the Atlantic.

In May 1907, in Pittsburgh, he leapt into the Allegheny River from what was then the Seventh Street Bridge (now re-named after native son Andy Warhol). In August he jumped into San Francisco Bay from a pier at the bottom of Washington Street. The next month, in Los Angeles, it was the lake in MacArthur Park (then known as Westlake Park): he jumped from the roof of a pavilion. In November he dove into the Mississippi from the gangplank of a steamboat moored near the Canal Street ferry terminal in New Orleans. On the last day of April 1908, in Boston, he leapt from the Harvard Bridge into the Charles River wearing a "cerise-colored bathing suit." Later that month, in Philadelphia, he jumped from the Market Street Bridge into the Schuylkill River. And in June in Portland, Maine, he leapt from the Portland Bridge (now known as the Casco Bay Bridge) into the Fore River. In September, on the other side of the ocean, he jumped from the elegant Friedrichs Bridge in Berlin into the murky Spree Canal. Three months later near Birmingham, England—in the dead of winter, in a heavy downpour—he jumped from a houseboat into the Edgbaston Reservoir. In April 1909, in Paris, he jumped into the Seine from the roof of the morgue on the Île de la Cité—and brought along a film crew to catch the action. In Scotland in June he leapt from a swing bridge at the entrance to the Earl Grey Dock in Dundee; three days later from the paddle steamer *Marchioness of Bute* into the river Tay; and a week after that from the tug *John McConnachie* into the channel of the harbor at Aberdeen, under very choppy conditions. In July he jumped off the Brighton Pier, and in August from the Stonehouse Bridge in Plymouth—"nude except for a pair of white knickers."

Heraclitus taught that no man ever steps into the same river twice, but there were certain aspects of Houdini's bridge jumps that were immutable: the crowds were huge, the handcuffs and leg irons heavy and cruel, the thrill palpable. And Houdini never failed to emerge from the water free.

5

Aloft Down Under

IN LATE AUGUST, a week after leaping in his white knickers off the Stonehouse Bridge, Houdini was on holiday in Reims, France, in the Champagne region. Like almost everybody in Europe that summer, he'd been caught up in the excitement generated by a momentous feat: a month earlier, on July 25, 1909, Louis Blériot became the first person to pilot an airplane across the English Channel. A new age was dawning and Harry, galvanized by the magic of flight, arranged to attend the Reims Aviation Week, a popular and glamorous event sponsored by the great Champagne houses. What he saw tightened the grip of a new enthusiasm: Harry was now determined to take to the air.

Or at least that's one of several versions of the story he liked to tell.

Another version has him catching his first glimpse of a flying machine two months later, in early November, during a nine-week engagement at the Hansa Theater in Hamburg.

Harry watched a German aviator circle in a Voisin biplane and land clumsily, whereupon the mysteriarch raced across the improvised airfield and peppered the startled pilot with questions: *How much for a plane like this? Where can I get one, and how soon?*

In yet a third version, also set near Hamburg, it was a French aviator Harry watched fly, and the plane—again a Voisin—caught fire in midair, forcing the pilot to bail out (a twenty-foot drop that caused only minor injury).

All three stories end happily, with Harry buying a Voisin biplane in Hamburg in mid-November, paying $5,000 for the privilege of becoming a pioneer aeronaut. At the same time he rented a hangar to house his aircraft and hired a French mechanic, Antonio Brassac, to teach him the fundamentals of flying and to look after the machine. Already obsolete by the time Harry bought it, the Voisin was a cumbersome craft made of wood, canvas, and wire, underpowered and unstable in a breeze—but relatively uncomplicated to fly.

Windy weather delayed his debut as a pilot; it wasn't until November 26 that the Handcuff King first slipped the surly bonds of earth and rose up into the sky. Not the triumph he'd hoped for, the flight was brief, the landing abrupt. His diary entry is a study in tight-lipped disappointment: "I smashed machine. Broke Propeller all to hell." Three days later he took out a $25,000 life insurance policy (a precaution he might have considered before jumping off a bridge in handcuffs).

Not in the least deterred by this bumpy beginning, he hatched a plan: he would combine his infatuation with flying with a forthcoming tour of Australia. He'd been offered $2,000 per week to play in Melbourne and Sydney, and the theater owner had offered to pay him during the long sea voyage as well—Harry couldn't resist the idea of being paid to travel. Now he had an added incentive: he would become the first person to make a successful flight Down Under.

On January 7, 1910, Houdini and his entourage (Bess, two

assistants, and Brassac the mechanic) and his equipment (including the Voisin, disassembled) boarded the RMS *Malwa* in Marseilles, bound for Adelaide. The journey lasted nearly a month, with stops along the way in Egypt (to pass through the Suez Canal), Ceylon, and Fiji. Harry was almost constantly seasick, and shed some twenty-five pounds as a result.

He was back in action almost as soon as he set foot on solid ground. Having disembarked in Adelaide on Saturday, February 5, he traveled the next day to Melbourne, a seventeen-hour train journey, and performed for the first time at the New Opera House on Monday—barely forty-eight hours into his Antipodean adventure. Ten days later, watched by many thousands who braved the broiling midday heat, he dove headfirst from Queens Bridge into the muddy Yarra River. His daily routine began at sunrise, when he was chauffeured out to Diggers Rest, twenty miles northwest of Melbourne, where Brassac was reassembling the Voisin at a makeshift airfield in a dusty paddock called Plumpton's Field.

The Australian summer was brutal. Houdini wrote in his diary on February 20, "Hottest day I ever lived. Must have been 119 in the shade and the wind was scorching. Drank enough water to float a rowboat." In the afternoon he was driven back into town in time to take the stage. His performance began with film footage of the Market Street Bridge jump in Philadelphia and the morgue jump in Paris. Then came Metamorphosis or the Milk Can trick, followed by the straitjacket escape. He accepted, as he had in America and Europe, a series of challenges: from carpenters who were eager to nail him up in a packing crate; saddlers who wanted to bind him to a workbench; and able-bodied seamen who were convinced that a good sailor's knot could never be unknotted. The performances were greeted with the usual rapture. The newspapers remarked on Houdini's American (!) accent and his "laboured enunciation."

Although the fuselage and the wings of the Voisin were

Houdini filled many exhibition dates in 1910.

9383—A.S.

fully assembled within days (the name HOUDINI blazoned in giant letters on the tail), the engine wasn't ready for nearly a month, a delay that frustrated Harry immensely. At last, early in the morning on March 18, he made three flights, the third of which lasted about three and a half minutes and covered two miles at a maximum altitude of a hundred feet. He admitted to feeling apprehensive during the preparations before take-off and while taxiing, but once the biplane was airborne he calmed down and enjoyed the "glorious thrill" of flight. In his diary he wrote, "Never in any fear and never in any danger." In the car on the way back to Melbourne, exultant, he told a reporter from the *Argus*, the local newspaper, "The funny thing was that as soon as I was aloft, all the tension and strain left me. When I was rolling, every muscle in me was taut. . . . In the air it's different. As soon as I was up, all my muscles relaxed, and I sat back, feeling a sense of ease. Freedom and exhilaration, that's what it is. O! she's great. I know what it is to fly in real earnest. She's like a swan. She's a dandy. I can fly." He was once again the Prince of the Air.

With a clutch of witnesses and photographic evidence to back him up, Houdini had met the criteria established by the Fédération aéronautique internationale (founded in 1905 to regulate the sport of flying) and was officially credited by the Aerial League of Australia—when it was established, a month after these daring aerial exploits—with making the first controlled, powered flight of an airplane in Australia. Which, as he explained to a reporter, was precisely what he was after: "I want to be first. I vehemently want to be first. . . . It is all I ask."

In fact he wanted more. With distance and endurance records to set, he was out at Diggers Rest the next day at dawn, staying airborne for nearly four minutes, a flight he described as "undoubtedly the best that I have made." The following day he improved on his personal best, remaining aloft for seven and a half minutes, which only egged him on. Once landed, he told his admiring audience, which by now had swollen to more than a hundred, that when conditions were right—a flat calm—he would attempt to keep his aircraft flying for a full thirty minutes. (It had taken Blériot a little over thirty-six minutes to cross the Channel.)

There would be no half-hour flights at Diggers Rest: Hou-

dini was booked for a five-week engagement at the Tivoli Theater in Sydney. He opened on Easter Monday, March 28, 1910.
The Voisin, which of course had to be dismantled to make the
five-hundred-mile trip, was put back together at the improvised airfield Harry rented at the Rosehill Gardens Racecourse
near Parramatta (about fifteen miles west of the Tivoli, which
was in the heart of Sydney). Once again Harry was commuting
between aviation and escapology.

In Sydney, as he had in Melbourne and Adelaide, he told
reporters that he planned to retire from the stage after his Australian tour—but now he explained that in his retirement he
would devote himself to aviation. His Tivoli performances were
almost exactly what he'd offered up at the Opera House in Melbourne, though he accepted fewer challenges. He announced
in the press that on April 14, 1910 (a little more than a week
after celebrating his thirty-sixth birthday), he would jump manacled into the Domain Baths, an enclosed saltwater pool on the
western side of Woolloomooloo Bay, less than a mile from
where the Sydney Opera House stands today. (He preferred
not to jump into the open harbor, he said, because he was afraid
of sharks.) This was his only open-air escape in Sydney—and
he charged 1 shilling admission. An audience of more than a
thousand watched from the grandstand as he leapt from the
second tier of the high-dive tower, thirty feet above the water.
Plunging headfirst, he botched his entry, giving himself two
black eyes—a painful blow, yet he endured it without betraying
any discomfort.

Three days later he disappointed a large crowd gathered at
Rosehill Racecourse to watch him fly: too much wind. The next
day he made three attempts, with little success—on the third
attempt he just about took off, bounced awkwardly, and came
down again hard, off-kilter, and was thrown from his seat onto
the racetrack turf, landing uninjured on his hands and knees.
On April 19 he made a few short flights and landed smoothly.

The press coverage of these latest attempts encouraged the owner of the Tivoli to advertise "Aviation Week at Rosehill Racecourse" in the local newspapers: "Mr. Harry Rickards at enormous expense has arranged with the great Houdini to give a series of public flights on his Voisin biplane." The first day of Aviation Week was canceled: high winds again. The next day the advertisement promised that tea would be served in the pavilion—by Mrs. Houdini. A final flight, on May 1, watched by as many as five hundred spectators, was full of dramatic ups and downs that made the audience gasp and cheer. Houdini declared it "the flight of my life."

Two days later he supervised the dismantling of the Voisin, which was crated up and shipped to England. Harry was exhausted. "It is time I had the biplane packed, or it would have given me nervous prostration. Have not had much sleep for two months, and now I seem to have lost the habit." He gave a farewell interview to a journalist from the Sydney *Daily Telegraph* in which the urge to confess his weariness battled with his natural inclination to brag and boast: "I am strong, as you see; strong in flesh, but my will has been stronger than my flesh. I have struggled with iron and steel, with locks and chains; I have burned, drowned, and frozen till my body has become almost insensible to pain; I have done things which I rightly could not do, because I said to myself, 'you must'; and now I am old at 36. A man is only a man, and the flesh revenges itself."

The peculiar five-month interlude ended on May 11 when Houdini, Bess, and the two assistants sailed from Brisbane aboard the SS *Manuka*, bound for Vancouver.

Harry never again piloted a plane after his Australian adventure. His passion for flying vanished as if by magic. He talked about it occasionally, planning grandiose airborne stunts, claiming that on his next British tour he would travel by air, hopping from city to city in his Voisin. Yet the biplane was never reassembled. It's possible that in his heart Harry disliked flying as much as he disliked driving—but the thought of being first, of holding a record, trumped his aversion. Aviation, for him, was another, less strenuous path to the American success he craved, a way to win applause of the kind that echoes through the ages. He imagined himself fêted and hailed as a hero, as Blériot was, or as Charles Lindbergh would be seventeen years later, after his solo transatlantic flight. If taking to the air was a viable shortcut to heroism, Harry was willing to risk it. And then at some point—maybe aboard the *Manuka*, the "miserable wretched looking steamer" alone in the vast Pacific—Harry stopped believing that flight would make him more famous than he already was.

6

The Great Dissolution

HOUDINI LOVED to tell a story about a private performance he staged for an audience of one. The performance had nothing to do with magic or the art of escape, and yet he called it the greatest thrill of his life. In June 1912, while playing at Hammerstein's Roof Garden, he asked to be paid his weekly salary in gold. At the end of the week he was handed a canvas sack heavy with double eagle gold coins and took it straight home to 278, into his mother's room. "Mother, Mother," he cried, "do you remember the promise I made Father years ago that I would always look after you? Look what I am able to bring you now! Hold out your apron!" He poured the coins, a tinkling golden cascade, into his mother's lap.

Is this fantasy, or did a thirty-eight-year-old man, rich and world famous, act out this operatic scene? It has the elemental simplicity of a fairy tale and embarrassingly obvious sexual connotations. In Harry's mind it was a grand gesture of filial piety—exhilarating, and as real as his ardent love for his mother.

He worried about her during his long absences, wrote to her faithfully, and went to extraordinary lengths to be with her whenever he could. In the summer of 1909, in the midst of an extended European tour, he paid for "the two mothers"—Bess's mother and Cecilia—to cross the Atlantic and join him in England for eight weeks. (In addition to paying their expenses, he gave them each $5 a day in pocket money.) Concerned for Cecilia's health during the sultry New York summers, he sent her to a resort in the Catskills for the mountain air. Parting, when he went on tour in Europe, became increasingly difficult for both mother and son. She took to telling him, as they said goodbye on a pier, that this was perhaps the last time they would see each another. She said it again at the Hoboken Docks on July 8, 1913, the day he sailed for Hamburg aboard the aptly named *Kronprinzessin Cecilie*—and in the same breath asked him to bring her back a pair of cozy woolen slippers, size 6. Houdini and Bess were en route to Scandinavia, with bookings in Denmark and Sweden. He was scheduled to perform for King Gustav V at the royal palace in Stockholm.

His brother Dash ("Hardeen, the Great Sensation of Two Hemispheres") was booked to appear at the Lyric Theater in Asbury Park, a seaside town on the New Jersey shore. As usual, he was borrowing from his brother's repertoire (straitjacket, Milk Can)—and he decided to bring Cecilia with him, thinking that she might enjoy an ocean breeze. They checked into the Imperial Hotel on Monday, July 14. In the evening Hardeen performed at the Lyric, and later that night Cecilia suffered a stroke. The examining doctor pronounced her condition serious and Dash summoned his sister Gladys and cabled Harry. But the show must go on: at noon the next day Hardeen jumped manacled into the Atlantic from an Asbury Park fishing pier;

he performed that evening and the next at the Lyric, rushing to his mother's sickbed as soon as the curtain came down. After Wednesday's performance, Cecilia tried to tell Dash something, a message she had for Harry, but her speech was garbled by aphasia. She died in the early hours of Thursday, July 17, 1913.

Houdini and Bess, meanwhile, had taken the midnight train from Hamburg to Copenhagen, arriving on the morning of July 16. They were greeted by Houdini's assistants, one of whom handed him a cable that he saw was from his family and blithely assumed was merely welcoming him to Europe; he put off reading it. At his performance that evening at the Circus Beketow, two princes of the Danish royal family were in the audience. The next day, Houdini attended a press reception at the Circus. As he was preparing to meet the assembled journalists, another cable was delivered. When he opened it, he fainted. Revived, he wept and cried out, "Mother—my dear little mother—poor little mama."

An unexpected blow, his mother's death made him physically ill. Back at the hotel, he lay on his bed suffering agonies of grief and also a familiar, debilitating pain. Two years earlier he had ruptured a blood vessel in his kidney while performing a full-body straitjacket escape—and now the doctor summoned by Bess confirmed that the pain was a symptom of chronic kidney disease, exacerbated by shock. The doctor recommended that the patient be hospitalized immediately. Harry of course refused. Instead he asked to be released from his contract with Circus Beketow and cabled Dash, instructing him to delay their mother's funeral. Bent on seeing Cecilia one last time, he booked passage back to New York—once more aboard the *Kronprinzessin Cecilie*, an irony no biographer could resist underlining.

By custom, Jewish burials take place as quickly as possible, usually a day or two after death. Postponing internment for nearly two weeks, as in this case, is an offense against tradition.

Yet Harry's siblings agreed to his demand. On July 29, when he arrived at 278, straight off the boat, he found his mother lying in state in the parlor. "She looked so dainty and restful," he wrote in his diary, "only a small spot on Her cheek." He sat with her all night. The next day she was buried next to her husband in the plot Harry had acquired in the Machpelah Cemetery in Queens. Also in the casket, slipped in by Harry during the long night's vigil, were the wool slippers he'd bought for her in Bremen before setting sail on his sad homeward journey.

After the funeral he stopped working for an entire month, during which he visited the grave nearly every day. When he wasn't at the cemetery he stayed home. He composed maudlin tributes to his mother, and had a photograph of her printed with the caption, "If God ever permitted an angel to walk the earth in human form, it was my Mother"; he sent these to friends, tucked into gloomy letters on black-bordered stationery. He mourned extravagantly, even after reluctantly going back on tour in Europe (again sailing for Hamburg, though not aboard the *Kronprinzessin Cecilie*). He read through the many letters his mother had written to him since 1900 ("each is a love story") and decided to have them transcribed and bound in book form. He wanted to see them "written in good German on typewriter"—that is, with the grammar tidied and the spelling corrected.

"I who have laughed at the terrors of death, who have smilingly leaped from high bridges, received a shock from which I do not think recovery is possible." Houdini was wrong about this: he did recover, in time. And yet the wild grief he experienced in the months after his mother's death faded only gradually and left behind a lasting residue of melancholy. Grief dogged him. Toward the end of November he wrote in his diary, "Am feeling a bit better, but July 17 is always on my mind." To his brother he confided, "Dash its TOUGH, and I cant seem to get *over it*. Some times I feel alright, but when a calm moment arrives I am as bad as ever." And again: "Dash, I knew that I loved Mother, but that my very existence seems to have expired with HER, is simply writing my innermost thoughts."

Also in his innermost thoughts was his own mortality, inextricably entwined with the sorrow caused by the "Great Dissolution"—his overwrought phrase for the death of his seventy-two-year-old mother. Harry was now thirty-nine and had driven himself relentlessly since he was a teenager, demanding of his body feats of strength and endurance simply unthinkable for a normal human being. The strain of being a superman was beginning to tell, and not just in his kidney. Bess noticed it as early as 1911; she wrote to Dash, "Harry is worked to death, he looks so old, he is quite gray." And Harry confessed as much in his diary: "Gee but its hard to keep at it all the time. . . . Very hard job." His mother's death made it even harder, in that he lost his zest for performance. Four months later he told Dash, "My brain works naturally, and I try and scheme ahead as in the Past, but I seem to have lost all ambition." Bereavement sapped his confidence and took a physical toll. He was no longer invincible, and acknowledging that fact hurt, emotionally and physically. He told himself, with some success, to snap out of it: "Must try and cheer up and be a man."

In December he canceled performances in Paris and headed south to Nice for a holiday with Bess on the Riviera. Eager to distract him from his grief, Bess gave him permission to gamble at the casino in Monte Carlo. He won but seemed less interested in his winnings than in a nearby cemetery reserved for those who committed suicide after gambling away their last penny. In his diary he wrote with undisguised fascination about this dismal graveyard.

When he returned from Europe in June 1914 he found he couldn't live in 278—the memory of his mother pervaded the brownstone and made what had been his home too sad to bear.

In August he and Bess moved in with Dash, into the top floor of his house in the Flatbush neighborhood of Brooklyn.

He sought solace in designing a magnificent memorial to his parents, a vast granite exedra blazoned with the name Weiss and decorated with a weeping figure carved from Italian marble, both the graven image and the opulence of the monument an offense against Jewish law and custom. The monument commemorated both his father and his mother—but the exedra, with its staggering $40,000 price tag, was commissioned only after Cecilia's death. Of course Harry intended to be buried there as well: *Houdini* would be carved in the granite above

Weiss. He was designing his own tomb, an activity entirely consonant with his mood.

* * *

"Must invent some new means of enlightening my labors," he wrote in his diary. One "enlightening" idea was to make magic the focus of his act rather than escapology—less wear and tear on his aging body. In early 1914, while touring in England, he put together a new show he called a Grand Magical Revue that he promised would reveal him as "the Greatest Mystifier that History Chronicles." The revue featured a number of tricks he had bought from other magicians, and some he copied shamelessly, all the while boasting that this would be the first time they would be seen on any stage. The opening act, for instance, was the Crystal Casket. Houdini threw gold coins into a glass box suspended over the center of the stage. The coins disappeared as they left his hand but landed all the same with a clatter in the coffer. The trick was filched—pilfered—from Robert-Houdin, the man Houdini had once called his "guide and hero" and later the "Prince of Pilferers." Later in the show Houdini made assistants disappear. He made them reappear. He produced—from thin air, as magicians like to say—hundreds of coins. He destroyed yards of calico, burning it, cutting it, then restored the cloth to pristine condition. Except for Metamorphosis, which he performed with Bess as a finale, none of this was what the audience wanted; theater managers, too, were unimpressed. Houdini—aka "the Supreme Ruler of Mystery"—insisted that his Grand Magical Revue was a triumph: "Best show I ever presented."

It was while he was absorbed in stage magic that he was given the idea for his most sensational open-air escape. The unlikely source was Randolph ("Randini") Douglas, a young Houdini imitator. An eighteen-year-old obsessed with locks and escapology, a devoted fan of the Handcuff King, Douglas had sought out his hero backstage after a show at the Empire Palace in Sheffield in April 1913. Impressed by Douglas's fervent admiration and his dedication to the art of escape, Houdini gave the teenager his blessing and his address. They struck up a correspondence, and fourteen months later, when Houdini was performing his Grand Magical Revue in Nottingham, he accepted an invitation to tea in Sheffield where Douglas lived in an attic room in his parents' house. The young man had a new trick he wanted to demonstrate for his famous guest. Up in the attic, Douglas asked Houdini to strap him into a strait-jacket, then sat down on the floor while his stepmother, Kitty, bound his ankles with a rope that ran through a pulley at the apex of the gabled ceiling to a winch on the wall. With Kitty's help, Houdini worked the winch, drawing the young man's feet up and up toward the pulley on the ceiling. When his head was hanging a yard or so above the attic floor, he wriggled out of the straitjacket with Houdiniesque ease, dropped it in a heap, and spread his arms wide. Houdini understood immediately that the forty-mile detour he'd taken by traveling from Notting-ham to this attic room in Sheffield had been entirely worth it.

The suspended straitjacket escape, Houdini-style—dan-gling high above a breathless lunchtime crowd, preferably in full view of the offices of a major newspaper—was still incu-bating when he sailed home at the end of June. Harry had booked passage on the SS *Imperator*, the largest passenger ship in the world at the time, and for once he was spared seasick-ness. Which was fortunate because he had planned a sensational act for his fellow passengers, one of whom, as he'd learned when he bought his ticket, was Theodore Roosevelt, recently returned from an arduous expedition to explore the Amazon basin. Determined to impress the Colonel, as the famously vig-orous and exuberant former president liked to be called, Hou-dini offered to jump manacled from the deck of the ship. The captain forbade it. Another idea, plotted in the weeks before the ship sailed, worked to perfection. Houdini maneuvered

Roosevelt into requesting a séance as part of the entertainment on the gala night, then arranged to have the "spirits" draw on a seemingly blank slate the answer to the Colonel's question ("Where was I last Christmas?"): a detailed map of the river Roosevelt had been exploring in the Brazilian rainforest. The audience was astonished, none more so than Roosevelt, who asked Houdini the next day whether he'd witnessed "genuine Spiritualism." "No, Colonel," Houdini replied, "it was just hocus-pocus." Years later, when he was crusading against the quackery of spirit mediums, Houdini revealed that he had acquired the map from a London newspaper that was preparing—but had yet to publish—an article by Roosevelt on his Amazon expedition. A brilliant coup, perfectly executed by a polished and resourceful showman, the mock séance was widely reported in the press and added a lick of presidential polish to Houdini's fame.

Another kind of magic produced a photograph of Harry and the Colonel standing side by side on the deck of the *Imperator*. Harry sent the photo to just about everyone he knew, as ocular proof that he and Roosevelt were friends. What he didn't say, and no one could see, was that five other people were standing with them in the original photograph. Harry had the others airbrushed from the picture; they vanished into thin air.

Several days after Harry landed in New York, the assassination in Sarajevo of Archduke Franz Ferdinand of Austria set the world on the path to disaster. In the tense month before the great powers declared war on one another, Harry zigzagged—as he would for the duration of the Great War—between arduous or risky escapes and stage magic that left no bruises on his body and his clothes in one piece. He was performing in July 1914 at Hammerstein's Roof Garden, and the strenuous Chinese Water Torture Cell was the featured act of the first week. The next week he unveiled a new effect he'd bought from a British magician a month earlier, Walking through a Brick Wall.

This trick required virtually no physical exertion, but the apparatus was large and costly: a brick wall, nine feet high and ten feet long. Houdini wore a white duster over his evening clothes to perform the trick, which simply involved him disappearing from one side of the wall (while concealed by a screen) and reappearing on the other side (again behind a screen). It was a hit, according to *Billboard* magazine: "The audience sat spellbound for fully two minutes after this feat was accomplished. They were too dumbfounded to applaud." On the same bill as Walking through a Brick Wall was the Double Fold Death Defying Mystery, an elaboration of the Milk Can escape, in which the milk can was locked inside a large wooden chest, an ingenious apparatus incorporating some of the trickery that made possible the Water Torture Cell escape. Houdini had learned that even if he could produce spellbinding, dumbfounding magic that posed no threat to life and limb, on the same bill he would have to defy death (and emerge soaking wet) to satisfy his audience.

To promote his run at Hammerstein's, he announced a "Daring Dive" off the Battery at the southern tip of Manhattan. The newspaper advertisement promised that rain or shine Houdini would be "handcuffed and leg ironed" and nailed up in a packing crate encircled by steel bands and weighed down with two hundred pounds of iron—and the crate would then be "thrown" into the river. It was all true, except that the crate was lowered with a winch, not thrown. Fifteen thousand spectators were on hand to see him survive yet again.

Although the conflagration on the other side of the Atlantic meant that Harry had to cancel his European engagements, and that he lost his assistant Franz Kukol to the German war effort, it otherwise had little effect on him until the spring of 1917 when the U.S. joined the Allies in their effort to defeat the Central Powers. The show must go on.

In Kansas City, Missouri, at noon on September 8, 1915,

© HOUDINI.
1914.

Dietz
N.Y.

Houdini performed his first suspended straitjacket escape. The feat was promoted by the *Kansas City Post*, and it was on the back of a flatbed truck parked on Main Street in front of the *Post* building that Houdini prepared himself for his ordeal. The newspaper estimated the crowd at five thousand. Two detectives strapped him into "the strongest straitjacket owned by the Kansas City police department." He was laid down on the bed of the truck, a thick rope was bound around his ankles, and he was hoisted twenty feet into the air, feet first. The crowd gave a cheer. From the *Post*'s eyewitness account:

> For a second Houdini hung motionless. Then he began to twist and turn and contort his agile body into strange postures. Suddenly his tightly bound arms seemed to loosen and slip downward. In another second one of the arms . . . slipped over his head.
>
> The other followed and in ten seconds the impregnable police "jacket" . . . slipped harmlessly over his head and fell to the sidewalk.
>
> Houdini was free.

The struggle lasted twenty seconds—a short show that left the citizens of Kansas City satisfied yet bewildered. "As the big throng dispersed," according to the *Post*, "each man asked his neighbor, 'How does he do it?' "

It's apparently somewhat easier to escape from a straitjacket when hanging upside down, but it's a tough physical challenge no matter how it's done. At the end of September, in Minneapolis, Houdini was hoisted forty-five feet in the air, and soon enough it was a hundred feet up—in Houston, Washington, DC, Baltimore, Boston. The added height allowed for a longer, more dramatic spectacle, and made the challenge riskier: both the journey up and the journey down presented dangers. The longer he was suspended, the greater the strain on his ankles. And finally there was the strain on his core muscles and the risk to his internal organs from the spasmodic thrashing and furious gyrations—witness the ruptured blood vessel in his kidney. Larger cities and higher elevations added up to bigger crowds. But the crowds were big all over the country: Salt Lake City, Oakland, Denver, Cincinnati, Grand Rapids, Atlantic City, Fort Worth.

While in Fort Worth in January 1916 he allowed himself to

be dragged behind a motorcycle, freeing himself from hand-cuffs in the process. A few weeks later, in San Antonio, where he performed another suspended straitjacket escape, he told an interviewer, "I don't know how long this thing can last. I have given myself from one to eight years, and that's a liberal esti-mate. I am now forty-two years of age. I feel like I am fifty-two years, and some of the time much older—just as I do this afternoon. I have been told it is the hardening of the arteries. Perhaps it is. Whatever it is I am getting old and yet I have no particular regrets. Some time or another we all grow tired. I have been tired for a long time."

Three months later a hundred thousand people turned up to watch his suspended straitjacket escape in the nation's capital. He was interviewed the day before by a reporter from the *Washington Times*; once again he threatened to stop putting his life on the line for the entertainment of urban mobs. The refrain was by now familiar: "I've about made up my mind that this is the last stunt I'll perform. Hereafter I intend to work entirely with my brain. See these gray hairs? They mean something. I'm not as young as I was. I've had to work hard to keep ahead of the procession. I'll still be entertaining the public for many years to come, but I intend to do it along lines not quite so spectacular. As an escapist extraordinary I feel that I'm about through." And yet a week later he was in Baltimore, dangling upside down in front of reporters peering through the windows of the *Baltimore Sun* building, a hundred feet above the intersection of Charles and Baltimore Streets.

Even as his outdoor stunts grew more outrageous (and his complaints about them louder), his stage magic grew more extravagant. The crowning moment came in early January 1918 at New York's colossal Hippodrome Theater. Houdini appeared as a guest act in a circus-themed variety show called *Cheer Up!* (the title an unsubtle attempt to lift the spirits of a nation whose troops were poised to engage in trench warfare on the western front).

On the vast Hippodrome stage, in front of an audience of more than five thousand, Houdini was a tiny, solitary figure. After his introductory remarks he was joined by Jennie, a large Asian elephant, who arrived at a fast trot, led by her trainer. The three-ton animal did a few rapid circles around the magi-

cian, saluted the audience with her trunk, gave Houdini a kiss, and accepted in turn a lump of sugar. Stagehands then dragged a large ghost cabinet on wheels to the center of the stage. The cabinet—the size of a short shipping container—was dressed up as a circus wagon with openings at both ends. The stagehands turned it so the audience could look through, then lowered a ramp for Jennie, who trotted all the way around the cabinet before lumbering up the ramp, led by her trainer. The curtains were drawn at both ends—and when they were opened again as the orchestra cymbals clashed, the elephant (and the trainer) had vanished. "You can plainly see," said Houdini with his exaggerated enunciation, "the animal is completely gone."

There are conflicting reports concerning the reaction inside the Hippodrome, which may well have been more muted than Houdini would have liked. (After all, only a fraction of the people in the audience had seats that allowed them to see through the cabinet to the backdrop; the rest had to take his word for it that the pachyderm was indeed "completely gone.") Reviews in the press, however, were exactly what he'd hoped for. *Variety* chose the headline "Houdini Hides an Elephant" and declared in the first sentence, "Houdini puts his title of premier escape artist behind him and becomes The Master Magician." *Billboard* made its point with alliteration, praising "Houdini's prodigious presentation of perfect prestidigitation." His run at the Hippodrome was extended to nineteen weeks, the longest of his career.

According to the theater's promotion, it was "The Most Colossal Disappearing Mystery that History Records," and according to Houdini himself, it was "the biggest vanish the world has ever seen"—but was it enough to make Houdini the Master Magician? Not according to his peers. The preeminent stage magician of the day was an elegant character called Howard Thurston. Five years older than Harry and possessed of a honeyed baritone voice and preternatural manual dexterity, Thurston was the anointed successor to Harry Kellar, the grand old man of American magic. Thurston toured the country with a huge, elaborate magic show, complete with animals, automata, and a troupe of chorus girls. Nothing he did onstage ever tousled his hair or rumpled his evening clothes. Audiences loved him, and so did the critics—no wonder Houdini was envious.

Despite his repeated attempts to claim the mantle of Master Magician, in the imagination of the multitudes he remained an escape artist. Though it wasn't yet in the dictionary (that would come in 1920, when his press agent convinced Funk & Wagnalls to include the word *Houdinize:* "To release or extricate oneself . . . as by wriggling out"), the word *Houdini* was already synonymous with escape. But because the death-defying stunts were elemental and their impact visceral, because his continued survival seemed incredible, he was credited with supernatural powers. This was different from stage magic, and different also from the occult effects at a séance. More than simply an entertainer or a medium, he seemed to be a kind of roving miracle worker.

And in the years before he launched his campaign against Spiritualism, he wasn't averse to letting the legend of his special powers spread. Witness a famous exchange with one of the few celebrities whose name was more widely recognized than his: Sarah Bernhardt.

A truly global superstar for more than three decades, the Divine Sarah embarked in 1916 on a farewell tour of the United States, magisterial on the stage even on one leg (the other having been amputated a year earlier). At the start of the tour, at the Metropolitan Opera House in New York, the actress was presented with a bronze statuette—and, embarrassingly, the bill for it. This fiasco leaked to the press and Houdini cannily stepped in and publicly announced that he would pay for the statuette, dispatching a check for $350 to the sculptor's widow. This grand gesture earned him a mountain of favorable news coverage (his clipping service counted more than three and a half thousand articles mentioning the incident), as well as the goodwill of the most celebrated woman in the world. Several weeks later they met in Boston, a celebrity summit of sorts. Houdini was invited up to Bernhardt's hotel room, where he entertained her with half an hour of magic tricks. The next day she accompanied him to the B. F. Keith Building on Tremont Street and watched him perform a suspended straitjacket escape. Afterward, in the car back to the hotel, the actress and the escapologist had their famous conversation. But we have only Houdini's inevitably self-serving version of what was said. The gist, according to him, is that Bernhardt asked him to please restore her amputated limb. "She honestly thought I was superhuman," he proudly told the press. When a New Orleans newspaper pointed out how improbable the story was, arguing that the notoriously savvy Bernhardt was hardly likely to make such a naïve request, Houdini bristled, shocked at the suggestion that he would ever feed a reporter "a misleading story."

In *Humboldt's Gift*, Saul Bellow has his narrator, Charlie Citrine, tell an exaggerated version of the story: "Bernhardt was already very old and her leg had been amputated. She sobbed and hung on Houdini's neck as they were driven away in the car and begged him to give back her leg."

The dubious anecdote lives on: the Divine Sarah asked Houdini to do the impossible—because that's what he did.

* * *

Six months before Jennie the elephant vanished, in June 1917, Houdini was elected president of the Society of American Magicians, an organization he'd joined in 1903 and with which he had a long and somewhat vexed relationship. He'd written for the society's magazine, and he'd served as its vice president. He'd hoped (in vain) that his own short-lived magazine, *Conjuror's Monthly*, might be adopted by SAM as its official organ. But his combative style and his spiteful book about Robert-Houdin had alienated some of the membership. When his plans for *Conjuror's Monthly* came to nothing, he resigned from the society in a huff, then some years later accepted an honorary membership. One source of the friction was Houdini's long-running, acrimonious feud with A. M. Wilson.

A Kansas City physician, Wilson was the editor of the *Sphinx*, which began as the "Western organ" of SAM and became the official organ in 1909. A magic traditionalist, Wilson considered escapology a lesser field of endeavor, and did the one thing guaranteed to rile Houdini: he ignored him. Snobbery seems to have played a part in Wilson's low opinion of Houdini, whom he described as "absolutely void of education and mental training." With some justification, Wilson believed that Harry was fundamentally unscrupulous, someone who would "betray his best friend for money or a page in a daily newspaper"—though in truth Harry was always less interested in money than publicity. As if he had made a dedicated study of how to wound his adversary, Wilson appealed to a traditional hierarchy, and consigned the escape artist to the lowest rung: "Magic is an art, a science that requires brains, skill, gentlemaness and talent of high order. Brick walls, torture cells, straightjackets, handcuffs, etc., demand nothing but physical strength and endurance, nerve, gall, bluster, fakes and fake apparatus, etc., ad libitum, heralded by circus band advertising. In my opinion, magic is brought into disrepute by all such. Their place is in the side show or dime museums." Telling Houdini that he lacked "gentlemaness" and that he belonged in a side-show was bound to provoke a reaction.

Houdini's jabs at Wilson were aimed at the doctor's age (he was eighteen years older than Harry) and relied on absurdly high-flying language clearly meant to refute the idea that he was an illiterate grifter who belonged in a dime museum: "A man of middle or old age, with the beautiful calling that gives him the knowledge to render succor to the sick, helpless and

dying ought not to allow envy and jealousy to stir him to be-
smirch his conscience and defile manhood and family in a use-
less endeavor to heap calumny upon the character of those of
younger blood whom he sees passing by him with giant strides."

It sounds like gibberish, but that's sometimes the noise the
ego makes when it's assailed in print. Wilson again: "Houdini
is yet a young man with much to learn. I am sorry for him that
money has become his god and self-conceit has caused him to
idolize himself." Harry made it known that anyone who wrote
for the *Sphinx* was no friend of his. He claimed to have in his
possession a list of hundreds of women with whom Wilson had
had "criminal relations as an adulterer and fornicator." The
feud continued for a decade.

And then, suddenly, they patched up the quarrel: after a
face-to-face meeting in Kansas City in September 1915, they
declared they were now friends. Harry could nurse a grudge,
but he could also forgive and forget.

The feud with Wilson ended some eighteen months before America declared war on Germany. Both developments
played a part in Houdini's election as president of SAM. The
backing of Wilson, who put Houdini on the cover of the *Sphinx*
in June 1916 and ran an adoring profile, was a major step, but
it was Houdini's tireless work on behalf of the war effort that
sealed the deal.

America's entry into the war turned many citizens overnight
into jingoistic patriots, hot for victory and intolerant of dissent.
Harry, whose fondness for all things German evaporated on
April 6, 1917, registered for the draft (age forty-three), lobbied
his fellow members of SAM to pledge the organization's loyalty
to President Woodrow Wilson, and volunteered to entertain
the troops at army camps around the country. He raised money
for the Red Cross, trained soldiers to escape from German handcuffs, sold vast quantities of Liberty bonds, and organized (with

Al Jolson and Irving Berlin) the Rabbis' Sons' Theatrical Benevolent Association to give benefit performances in support of the troops.

He organized a sensational benefit at the New York Hippodrome in aid of the families of the sixty-seven servicemen who died when the SS *Antilles*, an army transport ship, was torpedoed in the North Atlantic by a German U-boat. Houdini promoted the show with a suspended straitjacket escape in Times Square, dangling sixty feet above Broadway and Seventh Avenue from a derrick being used in the construction of the Times Square subway station.

The *Antilles* gala, held in November, raised some $10,000. Houdini acted as master of ceremonies and also performed the Water Torture Cell escape, but the evening's main event was the appearance onstage of the great Harry Kellar, who had retired ten years earlier, having passed the mantle to Howard Thurston. The only magician Houdini ever acknowledged as his superior, Kellar traveled from California to take part in the benefit. After his performance, Kellar was carried off the stage in a sedan chair, showered with yellow chrysanthemums along the way, while the audience sang "Auld Lang Syne." (It's a measure of Houdini's respect for Kellar that this display did not spark a fit of jealousy.)

With these good works on behalf of the nation, Houdini, now president of SAM, made room for himself at the heart of the magic establishment—but other interests were dividing his attention. He had found a way to reach an even wider audience: the silver screen beckoned.

7

Making Movies

IT SEEMED at first a perfect match: Hollywood and Houdini would conspire to make money and spread his fame. The thrill of his greatest feats would be preserved on celluloid, the authenticity of the performance verified by the camera. His handsome face would become as famous as his name. The Houdini brand would be established worldwide and a burgeoning industry would add another star to its rapidly expanding firmament. As American audiences turned from the vaudeville theater to the cinema, would-be moguls imagined a global phenomenon: Houdini performing hairsbreadth escapes on screens in Japan, China, India, Brazil. The dashing hero could see it, too. There would be no limit to Houdini's fame. Here was a foolproof path to success.

He'd already appeared in several moving pictures, short documentaries recording outdoor stunts such as his 1907 jump from Weighlock Bridge. As early as 1909, Cinema Lux, a

French company, stitched together a series of stunts and made a feature film called *Merveilleux exploits de Houdini à Paris* ("The Marvelous Exploits of Houdini in Paris"), which survives only in fragments. But he didn't become deeply involved in the film industry until 1916, the year after the stunning success of D. W. Griffith's *The Birth of a Nation*, when suddenly motion pictures seemed poised to eclipse vaudeville. Harry was approached about playing Captain Nemo in a film version of Verne's *Twenty Thousand Leagues under the Sea*, an idea that came to nothing but inspired him to write (and copyright) a film treatment entitled "The Marvelous Adventures of Houdini: The Justly Celebrated Elusive American." The title alone deserves an Oscar, but alas, the story, a nonstop action roller coaster, never made it to the screen. At the same time he was in negotiations to launch a new business tied to the movie industry. In September he invested $4,900 in a company, Film Developing Corporation (FDC), that he started with a German inventor, Gustav Dietz, who had patented a process for developing film for motion pictures. The FDC had offices in Manhattan and a factory in West Hoboken, New Jersey, and within a couple of years it was processing as much as a million feet of film per week.

The FDC was Houdini's first foray into the world of business. It was not a success. His company required regular infusions of cash and never turned a profit. It was also a drain on his time and energy. Eventually he convinced his brother Dash to give up performing as Hardeen and take over the management of the troubled enterprise. Then came the lawsuits and countersuits, and real-estate shenanigans involving holding companies. The mess dragged on for a half dozen years, giving Dash ulcers and Harry the enduring heartache of entrepreneur's remorse: "I have over 100,000 dollars invested in the F.D.C.," he wrote to Harry Kellar toward the end of 1920, "but have never received a penny from same. This does not include the many weary months I spent in and around the place trying to make a success of what an ordinary man in the business would have known was a failure. My education is certainly costing me a high price." Kellar owned 125 shares of FDC stock, which he eventually sold for $1—to Harry's sister, Gladys.

"The only good of the whole thing," Houdini wrote to Kellar as the FDC saga came to its untidy end, "is that it was the cause of my going into pictures." The first of those pictures was a fifteen-part serial called *The Master Mystery*, in which Houdini plays Quentin Locke, an undercover agent of the Justice Department investigating a malevolent corporation—International Patents, Inc.—for antitrust violations. The movie was made by a collection of industry veterans assembled by B. A. Rolfe, a vaudeville musician turned movie producer. Almost everyone involved, with the notable exception of Harry, had been working in and around movies for several years—in other words, from the early days of the motion picture industry. Harry received no credit for the screenplay, though he claimed to have collaborated on it with the pair cited as the authors, Charles Logue and Arthur B. Reeve. Among the projects Reeve had worked on was *The Exploits of Elaine*, a melodrama in the style of the highly successful *The Perils of Pauline*, which provided the cliffhanger template for *The Master Mystery*. Shot in a studio in Yonkers, New York, the film is a vehicle for Houdini's escapes: every time Locke turns a corner or walks through a door he is set upon by the same mercenary gang of thugs, and though he fights valiantly, they always wrestle him to the ground and tie him up in a straitjacket or a fishing net, or wrap him in barbed wire, or strap him into an electric chair. Instead of finishing him off right away, the gang leaves him to face his encroaching doom. Locke invariably pulls a Houdini—in one striking instance using his toes to free himself.

There's more to the movie, including an evil Automaton (the silver screen's first robot), a clunky backstory set in Mada-

gascar, a turbaned Madagascar native, expert in strangulation, and a love interest for Houdini named Eve, who's repeatedly kidnapped by the gang or menaced by the Automaton. The whole point is escape. Once Eve is kidnapped and Locke trussed up and facing certain death, the screen goes blank and up comes the card announcing, "The continuation of the HOUDINI SERIAL will be shown at this theater NEXT WEEK." A week later Houdini wriggles and thrashes his way to safety so that he can rescue Eve, the damsel in distress—at which point the cycle begins again.

The Master Mystery was a hit with audiences when the first episodes were released in November 1918, a hit with Houdini (who declared, "the Houdini Serial is the greatest ever screened"), and a hit with the critics. *Billboard* raved about the "crackerjack production." The timing was good: the war in Europe was over, and the nation was in the mood to celebrate. By the end of the year Harry was happily boasting, "The Movie Fans are 'clambering' for another Houdini serial, and as that is much easier than my Self created hazardous work, I may step that way." Actually, filming was hazardous, too: he fell during one of the many fight scenes and fractured his left wrist, a complicated break that had to be reset. And the business side of the industry was as slippery then as it is today. Although he'd been promised half the net profits (in addition to a weekly salary of $1,500), he eventually had to sue to get his share. The court case dragged on for four years; by the time he was awarded $33,000, the production company was bankrupt.

Hooked on film, Houdini signed in early 1919 with Famous Players–Lasky Corporation (FP–L), a major producer of silent movies run by the ruthless Adolph Zukor (like Harry an immigrant from Hungary). Zukor, who presided over Paramount Pictures for half a century, had assembled an impressive stable of stars at FP–L, including Mary Pickford, Gloria Swanson, and Rudolph Valentino. Houdini was offered a weekly salary of $2,500 plus a percentage of the profits.

The first of the FP–L movies was a murder mystery entitled *The Grim Game*. Arthur Reeve again wrote the screenplay, this time in collaboration with John W. Grey and Houdini himself, who claimed to have done the lion's share of the writing but once more received no credit for his contribution. The filming—in Hollywood—began in May and finished in July, briefly interrupted when Harry once again broke his wrist. As far as he was concerned, the rebroken bone was the only mishap: *The Grim Game* turned out to be the best Houdini vehicle, an altogether more sophisticated, polished, and coherent production than *The Master Mystery*. Houdini plays Harvey Hanford, a cheerful newspaper reporter who frequently flashes an exaggerated grin. Hanford is a regular guy, save for his inexplicable talent as a self-liberator. (After Quentin Locke, Houdini always played characters with the initials H. H., which surely helped the audience figure out where the escape artist skills came from.) Hanford is framed for a murder and thrown in prison and a gang kidnaps his fiancée, but of course it all works out in the end.

Thrill after thrill was packed into the seventy minutes of *The Grim Game*, including a suspended straitjacket escape and an awkward encounter with a bear trap. But the most astonishing stunt was a midair crash between two airplanes while Harvey Hanford was trying to scramble from one plane to the other. The collision was accidental, and could easily have proved fatal for the stuntman performing in Houdini's place. The footage of the crash is spectacular, as was the tall tale Houdini subsequently told about his involvement. "I was 3,000 feet up in an aeroplane, circling over another machine," he told *Picture Show* magazine, the stuntman having been forgotten by the time the star was interviewed. "I was dangling from the rope-end ready for the leap. Suddenly a strong wind turned the lower plane upwards, the two machines crashed together—nearly amputating my limbs—the propellers locked in a deadly embrace, and we were spun round and round and round." By a miracle he managed to "escape unhurt." In truth, divine intervention wasn't necessary: Harry never left the ground. His *Picture Show* account was perhaps the most brazen lie in a career that accommodated many, many whoppers.

The Grim Game was another hit, though *Variety* sounded an ominous note with a passing remark (perhaps inspired by news of a stunt double injured after a midair collision) about the filming of Houdini's escapes: "No one is certain he is doing what he seems to do."

A second FP–L film, *Terror Island*, most of it filmed in late 1919 on Catalina Island, twenty-odd miles off the California coast, was a shambles. Though written by the same team of Reeve and Grey, it's a limp and muddled adventure story about a coffer full of diamonds and an angry tribe of South Sea natives. Houdini plays Harry Harper, an inventor and philanthropist who spends most of his time aboard a submarine he designed himself. His plan is to use his submarine to recover sunken treasure—not for personal gain but to lift street urchins out of poverty. In the film's least plausible episode, Harry's love interest, a petite brunette with long dark tresses, is stuffed by the angry natives into an iron combination safe and hurled off a cliff into the water. With Harry's help she manages to "escape unhurt" from the safe, which has settled on the ocean floor. Unfortunately, this moment of high drama caused the audience, according to *Variety*, "to laugh outright."

Poor reviews, tepid box office, and the cold shoulder from Zukor, who declined to sign him up for a third FP–L film, did nothing to dampen Houdini's enthusiasm for the motion picture industry. On the contrary, within months of the release of *Terror Island* he plunged right back in, forming his own production company, the Houdini Picture Corporation, with the stated

HOUDINI PICTURE CORPORATION
presents

HOUDINI

"The MAN FROM BEYOND"

intention of making four full-length films a year, all starring Harry Houdini.

Shot at a studio in Manhattan and on location in Lake Placid, New York, and Niagara Falls, and released in April 1922, *The Man from Beyond* begins inauspiciously with pious sermonizing about reincarnation, the "promptings of a higher sense," and a close-up of an open Bible showing a verse from the Gospel of John about the imminence of the Second Coming. What follows is ponderous melodrama that builds slowly, slowly to a climactic rescue scene at Niagara Falls.

Houdini wrote the screenplay by himself, and was clearly hoping to ride the wave of Spiritualism's postwar resurgence. He plays Howard Hillary, who is brought back to life after having been frozen for a hundred years in a block of ice. (In France the film was given the title *L'homme du passé*, "The Man from the Past.") In his previous life Hillary had loved a woman named Felice, and now he loves an apparently reincarnated Felice in his new life. Not unsurprisingly, his professions of fervid devotion earn him a trip to the lunatic asylum. After his escape (the only escape of the movie), after the usual abductions and dust-ups, and after the watery excitement at Niagara, the soul of the long-dead Felice enters the body of the living Felice just before she and Howard share a final kiss. Sandwiched between them as their lips meet is a copy of Arthur Conan Doyle's Spiritualist manifesto, *The New Revelation*. Unimpressed, *Variety* pronounced the picture "pretty unsatisfactory" and pointed out what perhaps should have been obvious all along, that "melodrama and screen uplift won't mix."

Reviews of the Houdini Picture Corporation's next offering, *Haldane of the Secret Service*, were generally damning, but *Variety*'s pan must have been particularly wounding: "Perhaps the renown of Houdini is fading, or more probably the Broadway managers were wise to how bad a film this is." The poorly attended premiere did not, after all, mark the beginning of the end of his show business career. But the movie is terrible. Houdini plays Heath Haldane, a Secret Service agent in pursuit of a gang of counterfeiters who've killed his father, who was also a secret agent. The murderous gang has obscure ties to China ("mother of mystery and the black arts of necromancy behind her yellow veil of secrecy") in the guise of two sinister characters, Fuh Wong and Dr. Yu, who possess "all the craft and sinister cunning of the Far East." Again, there's a love interest, so Haldane is chasing a pretty girl and the bad guys at the same time. Houdini directed the film, his first and only attempt at direction, and the result is incoherent nonsense. The plot is the dramatic equivalent of the racist gibberish about China. Wandering senselessly from Shanghai to New York to London to Paris (with a stopover in Hull, England), the film looks as if it had been hastily assembled from a random assortment of outtake reels. The climax, such as it is, takes place in a monastery in the French countryside, with the counterfeiters dressed up as monks. Here Houdini makes his big escape—from a spinning water mill, an exciting few seconds before the denouement and the excruciating final kiss.

Haldane of the Secret Service marked the sorry end of Houdini's movie stardom. His ambitions thwarted, he quickly changed tack, moving on to the next thing with the tireless determination he brought to all his endeavors.

So what went wrong? Nearly everything. Thanks to the cinema, he was now famous all around the world. And yet with hindsight it's obvious that the medium itself was a disaster for an escape artist, for the simple reason that in a cleverly edited action sequence anybody could "pull a Houdini." The impossible, hitherto Houdini's private domain, became accessible to all—thanks to the camera. "*No* illusion is good in a film," he admitted at the end of his brief stint in the movie business, "as we simply resort to *camera* trix, and the deed is did." As the audience caught on to the possibility of trickery—the heroine with the long tresses wasn't really inside that safe plummeting from the cliff—it became glaringly apparent that the magic of the moving picture killed the magic of the escape artist. So Houdini went back to doing live suspended straitjacket escapes, dangling above major thoroughfares, in front of newspaper buildings—no "trix" at all.

To this day some Houdini fans maintain that his acting (especially in *The Grim Game*) wasn't all that bad. It was never any good. His handsome face—white with powder, eyes and lips accentuated by makeup—still made an impact, though his looks were less dazzling than they had been in his youth. His features were strong and appealing, but his curly hair was thinning, scraggly at times, and the hint of a jowl had softened his jawline. On a movie poster he could perhaps pass as a matinee idol, but on-screen, when the script called for the expression of some emotion, his face remained locked in place, a fixed stare with no suggestion of suppressed sentiment. Fear, rage, love,

P 257-11

heartbreak—whatever it was Houdini was meant to express, on-screen, it resembled dogged resolve, a blank visage that couldn't even be called enigmatic. Occasionally a rictus grin suggested mirth complicated by bitter irony (a twist surely absent from the script). In all his movies, he looked like the odd man out, isolated not by his daring (alone on the high truss of a bridge, about to jump) but because of his inability to act. He was an amateur with meager talent surrounded by professionals, and the difference was instantly apparent. "With all due respect to his famed ability for escapes," *Variety* sniped in the death knell review of his last film, "the only asset he has in the acting line is his ability to look alert."

* * *

His adventures in the moving picture business cost him more money than he earned, and might have sapped the confidence of someone without his armor-clad ego, yet he seems on the whole to have enjoyed his Hollywood interlude. He and Bess rented a modest bungalow and took the opportunity to hobnob with the stars, among them Charlie Chaplin, Gloria Swanson, and Fatty Arbuckle. He met the grown-up Buster Keaton, who had made his name as Arbuckle's sidekick and was beginning to star in films on his own. The proximity of the famous pleased Harry; he valued the celebrity of others nearly as much as his own.

In June 1919, soon after settling in Hollywood, he organized a lavish party to celebrate the twenty-fifth anniversary of his marriage, a white-tie dinner in the ballroom of the Hotel Alexandria in Los Angeles. He seated his guests at a long flower-laden table and served them a ten-course feast well lubricated with champagne. Harry and Bess made their entrance to the tune of Mendelssohn's Wedding March. Will Rogers was among those who delivered a toast to the happy couple. After dinner there was dancing until midnight, and Harry passed Bess a note: "If only my Sainted Mother were here, how she would nod her head with pride."

The extravagant and very public celebration of their silver wedding anniversary capped a fraught period in their marriage. "Been having a hard time with my private affairs," Harry wrote to a friend in February 1918. He was likely referring to what appears to have been his only adulterous affair, a perplexing episode that at first seems out of character. Prudish, uxorious

Harry really did cheat on Bess, but the experience, however disruptive at the time, merely reaffirmed his essential nature. As far as we know, he never deviated again, remaining prudish and uxorious till the end—a reminder of how hard it is to liberate oneself from the habits of a lifetime.

It all began in Oakland in the fall of 1915. On Tuesday, November 22, Harry had a busy day. At noon he was hoisted up in front of the First National Bank building at Broadway and 14th Street, where the offices of the *Oakland Tribune* were then housed. It was rainy and windy and the guide rope slipped as he was being winched up and he banged against the side of the building, striking his head. Then, after he'd freed himself from the straitjacket with the usual frenetic gyrations, it was discovered that the ropes had tangled, jamming the pulley; it took eight minutes, a long wait when you're dangling upside down, to get it working again. He told a *Tribune* reporter, "The blow on the head I did not mind so much—one gets used to hard knocks—but the trouble with the ropes was different. . . . My limbs were throbbing painfully, and one of them was bandaged from a previous accident at the time. I was a pretty sick man by the time they got that tackle working. I don't blame the men, of course, they were not used to the thing, but I'm mighty glad I am free again."

Free and back on solid ground, Harry scooted over to 12th Street for a matinee performance at the Orpheum Theater. After the show, two visitors, Jack London and his wife Charmian, were ushered backstage to meet him. World famous thanks to a pair of enduringly popular novels, *The Call of the Wild* (1903) and *The Sea-Wolf* (1904), as well as a steady stream of short stories published in widely read magazines, London was the first major literary celebrity Harry had ever encountered. When the Londons invited him for dinner at their favorite restaurant, he happily accepted. Jack and Charmian, his second wife, had been married since 1905, living on a thousand-acre ranch in Sonoma

County, forty-odd miles north of Oakland. Constantly active and politically engaged, they were proudly bohemian and vigorously unconventional. They clearly enjoyed both Harry's performance and the meal afterward because they returned the next day and again invited Harry out to dinner; this time Bess came along. The following day was Thursday the 24th, and Harry and Bess returned the Londons' hospitality by inviting them to Thanksgiving dinner in their hotel room. Also invited were Dash (in Oakland performing as Hardeen and pretending—in public at least—to be Houdini's archrival) and the vaudeville mogul who owned the chain of West Coast theaters where Hardeen was appearing. Photos were taken of the Houdinis with the Londons, and also of Jack and Harry on their own—Harry had no need to airbrush the image before sending it off to friends to boast about his friendship with a celebrated literary figure.

The next week, by which time the Houdinis had moved on to Los Angeles, Charmian sent Harry an inscribed copy of her book, *The Log of the Snark*, an account of the Londons' South Pacific voyage aboard their forty-five-foot ketch. She noted in her diary that she had met "Charming Houdini" and added, "Shall never forget him."

Although he was a robust and energetic man with a taste for adventure, Jack London suffered from poor health, the consequence of hardships endured as a youth in the Klondike gold rush, tropical diseases picked up aboard the *Snark*, and a lifetime of heavy drinking. After he returned in the summer of 1916 from an eight-month trip to Hawaii, his kidneys began to fail. Shocked by newspaper reports of his death, Harry cabled Charmian asking if it could possibly be true. It was: London died a year to the day after meeting Houdini backstage at the Orpheum. He was forty years old (two years younger than Harry), and the proximate cause of death was uremia.

Some fourteen months later, on January 17, 1918, Harry was

performing in *Cheer Up!* at the Hippodrome, making Jennie the elephant vanish. In the audience was the widowed Charmian, evidently no longer in mourning, wearing a white dress fringed with white fur. In town for a three-month visit, she was living, as any good bohemian would be, in Greenwich Village. Houdini had sent her tickets to the show, and afterward she came backstage to see him. He complimented her on her outfit and told her she looked like a young girl (she was forty-six); she in turn told her diary that he was as charming as ever. After several days of flirtatious notes and one "wonderful" telephone conversation, Charmian returned to the Hippodrome to see a second performance. It was only after she'd seen a third performance, sitting this time in the front row, that the affair began in earnest with Harry's visit to her apartment on Washington Place, an assignation that left her "stirred . . . to the deeps."

What we know of the affair comes almost entirely from Charmian London's diary, some of which is written in code, undecipherable except for the numerals "278," Harry's 113th Street address. (Harry and Bess moved back into the brownstone in February, while the affair was in full swing.) London refers to her "Magic Lover," "Magic Man," and "HH," and records (unencrypted) many of his passionate declarations. Though she was clearly excited by the liaison—"swept" is her preferred term—she kept her head. This was not a case of a lonely widow seeking solace: Charmian had many friends and lovers, and was carrying on with the active life she'd known with Jack. Harry, however, was full of romantic sentiment. He told her, "Now I know how kings have given up their kingdoms for a woman." He told her she was gorgeous, that he loved her. He told her, "I give *all* of myself to you." And the ultimate gauge of his feelings: "I would have told her—my mother—about you."

There's no way of knowing for certain what spark ignited the affair, but it seems likely that Charmian was the instigator.

As a young woman she had decided that passion and sex were creative urges and resolved to "love dangerously." As tall or taller than Harry, with a bright, toothy grin and a full figure, she was feminine but not dainty, womanly in ways the elfin Bess was not. No leap of faith is required to imagine Charmian London making her desires known and acting on them.

The lovers met for a handful of trysts over the course of a couple of months. Then Harry pulled back. Her diary records a series of disappointments: "Expect HH, but no word"; "Still no word on phone from H. Can't understand it." He was busy. He was of two minds. And he certainly wasn't about to give up his kingdom for another woman. The trysts came to a halt, but the passionate prose flowed on. When she was safely back in California, on the ranch in Glen Ellen (which she worked to preserve as a monument to Jack London), Harry sent her a stream of love letters, and sometimes telephoned to whisper sweet nothings in her ear.

They plotted reunions that never came to pass. After one

such disappointment she weighed Harry up in her diary: "Cautious Soul," she wrote.

* * *

In between the filming of *Terror Island* and the formation of the Houdini Picture Corporation, Houdini embarked on what would be his final trip abroad, a six-month tour of Great Britain, mostly honoring contracts signed before the war. Arriving with Bess in Southampton on January 5, 1920, he played big cities (London, Edinburgh, Glasgow) and small (Bradford, Nottingham, Hull), filling theaters wherever he went. His fame had spread appreciably, and the packed houses meant that the new contracts he negotiated were remarkably generous. In early May he played the London Palladium for a fortnight for the record-setting sum of $3,750 per week.

Compared with his prewar tours, this was easy money. The performance consisted of one escape, the Water Torture Cell, and a long monologue trumpeting his various exploits, with emphasis on cinema stardom. He wrote to a friend, "It's wonderful to think that after all my hard work, I can draw the Public without killing myself."

But the audiences who flocked to see the moving picture star were not always thrilled by the half-hour show on offer. In Nottingham a critic's complaint was especially blunt: "Why on earth Houdini should imagine that any audience would be entertained by hearing a long and uncalled-for account of what he had been doing for the last six years I am at a loss to understand. . . . People go to a Vaudeville house to see a performance . . . not to hear a diatribe on the personal pronoun worked around 'the story of my life, sir.'"

As usual, he was deaf to the criticism, which was in any case largely drowned out by adulation, both public and private. At the beginning of February the Magician's Club, which he'd founded (and largely funded) in 1913, and of which he was still president despite a six-year absence, held a banquet in his honor at the Savoy in London. The grateful membership presented him with a substantial silver box.

In several of the cities he visited, including Hull and Paris (where he flew with Bess for a week in late June aboard an early passenger plane), he filmed location scenes for movies that otherwise didn't yet exist, not even in his head. These street scenes were later used in the hodgepodge *Haldane of the Secret Service*.

Harry and Bess sailed home in early July aboard the *Imperator*. On this, his last voyage on an ocean liner, he was not seasick. He gave a shipboard performance—a charity benefit—doing magic but billing himself as "the World Famous Movie Star." He also began thinking about a new project, an idea for a book that took root in England after he'd made the acquaintance of Sir Arthur Conan Doyle—a "literary titan," Harry called him, as "justly famous as myself." Improbably, it was the creator of the great detective Sherlock Holmes, that paragon of cold, clear logic and rational deduction, who encouraged Harry to explore the murky faith-based realm where the next and final phase of his career would play out: the hushed, darkened séance chambers of the resurgent pseudo-religion, Spiritualism.

8

Among the Spirits

ON APRIL 14, 1920, halfway through his UK tour, when he was performing at the Brighton Hippodrome, Harry traveled to Crowborough, East Sussex, a journey of about twenty-five miles, to have lunch at Windlesham Manor, the Edwardian country house where Sir Arthur and Lady Conan Doyle (his second wife, Jean Leckie) lived with their three young children. This first meeting was sequel to a lively correspondence (ten letters in a fortnight) that began after Harry, promoting his tour and himself, sent Conan Doyle a copy of *The Unmasking of Robert-Houdin*. Spiritualism was the principal topic of the letters—specifically the spirit phenomena produced half a century earlier by the Davenport Brothers, who were revered by Spiritualists everywhere. In *The Unmasking*, Houdini had noted that the Davenports confessed that "all their work was skillful manipulation and not spiritualist manifestations"—to which Conan Doyle, who considered the brothers "probably the greatest mediums of their kind," politely objected. Eager for the celebrated author's friendship, and fully aware of his wholehearted belief in Spiritualism, Houdini equivocated, presenting himself as agnostic; he was, he insisted, "seeking truth."

Eleven days after the lunch at Windlesham, on Conan Doyle's recommendation, he attended a séance in London with a clairvoyant medium, Anna Brittain. Unimpressed, Harry confided in his diary: "All this is ridiculous stuff." And yet he claimed that in the remaining twelve weeks of his tour he attended more than a hundred séances—classic Houdini hyperbole that nevertheless contains a nugget of truth. A new compulsion had taken hold: he would write a history of Spiritualism. And though he wouldn't dream of saying so to Sir Arthur (and perhaps couldn't yet admit it to himself), his energy was already focused on exposing the "miracles" mediums produced in séances, a serial debunking prosecuted with the combative passion he'd brought to *The Unmasking*. This time, however, the unmasked and their allies—including Sir Arthur—would fight back.

Arthur Conan Doyle was so emphatically the perfect English gentleman that it comes as no surprise to learn that he was to a degree self-invented: he was born, raised, and educated in Scotland, not England, and his parents were both of Irish Catholic descent. A physician before he devoted himself full-time to writing, he was an avid sportsman with a particular fondness for cricket, golf, and skiing. Big and burly, with a long, luxurious English mustache that partially concealed a broad, kindly face, he was as physically unlike his new friend Houdini as possible. Fifteen years older and nearly a foot taller, he was vigorous and lively—yet calm and poised in comparison with the tense and impatient Houdini. One wag has pointed out that side by side they resembled Pooh and Piglet. They were unalike in character, too. Sir Arthur was proper and principled (and occasionally self-righteous), a resolute and resourceful advocate for fair play with a passion for righting wrongs: he was

twice successful in exonerating prisoners unjustly incarcerated by the British criminal justice system. Scrupulously courteous and fatally credulous, he was "as nice and sweet," said Harry, "as any mortal I have ever been near." Though he understood the value of publicity, and even had a talent for self-promotion, Sir Arthur was never boastful.

For all their differences, Conan Doyle and Houdini had certain things in common. Having each grown up with an absent and ineffectual father and a mother to whom he was conspicuously devoted, both developed early on a sturdy self-belief and an irresistible determination to succeed. Like Harry, Arthur was quick witted, curious, and intellectually ambitious (though unlike Harry he was well educated, so had a healthy head start). Both were powerful personalities, tenacious, not shy about broadcasting their opinions, and not inclined to tolerate contradiction. Most of these shared traits made their friendship, which grew gradually over the next couple of years, potentially volatile. They were drawn to each other for complicated reasons in which celebrity played a key role—and their celebrity meant that their every interaction, whether friendly or antagonistic, was scrutinized in the press.

The relationship was fueled in large part by Conan Doyle's dedication to Spiritualism. Like most Britons, he had lost family in the Great War and the influenza pandemic that followed. A son by his first marriage, Kingsley, was badly wounded in the neck at the Somme in the summer of 1916; two years later he succumbed to influenza, as did Sir Arthur's younger brother. Lady Conan Doyle lost a brother at the battle of Mons. Both husband and wife were certain they could make contact with the spirits of their dead kin. Anna Brittain, the medium Harry dismissed as ridiculous, put Arthur in touch with Kingsley soon after his death; the son assured the father he was happy beyond the grave. At a séance a year later Conan Doyle again made contact with Kingsley: "I said, 'Is that you, boy?'" he later wrote. "He said in a very intense whisper and a tone all his own, 'Father!' and then after a pause, 'Forgive me!'" Conan Doyle interpreted that last remark as his son's apology for not having shared his faith in Spiritualism.

Well before he met Houdini, Conan Doyle was already thoroughly invested in the world of the supernatural. It was his "sacred cause": he believed that he had been divinely appointed to be a "torch bearer." He even went so far as to suggest that the invention of Sherlock Holmes was foreordained, that the great detective was a means to an end: Holmes made Conan Doyle famous so that he could more easily spread the gospel of Spiritualism. He did so in two books published in the immediate aftermath of the war, *The New Revelation* and *The Vital Message*, which mapped out his conception of humanity's "new relations with the Unseen." Conveniently, his wife developed mediumistic powers, with a special talent for automatic writing: in a trance, Lady Conan Doyle became a conduit for the voices of the dead, their messages spelled out on the page in her rushed, angular handwriting. Just months after first meeting Houdini, Conan Doyle demonstrated the astonishing depths of his credulity by endorsing as genuine the Cottingley Fairies, sprites supposedly caught on camera by two young girls, cousins who lived in the West Yorkshire village of Cottingley. The photos purported to show fairies, cute little winged creatures, frolicking with the girls near a brook in the garden behind the older cousin's house. In truth, as the girls confessed decades later, the pixies were painted cardboard cutouts inspired by a popular children's book. Unmoved by a chorus of voices crying fraud, Conan Doyle championed the authenticity of the photographs in two magazine articles and then a book, *The Coming of the Fairies.* His hope was that recognition of the fairies' existence would "jolt the material twentieth century mind out of its heavy ruts in the mud, and . . . make it admit that there is a glamour and mystery to life"—glamour and mystery supplied by the supernatural.

He felt that Houdini's escapes, properly understood as supernatural phenomena, would have a similarly uplifting effect on benighted materialists. He was thrilled by the magic tricks his guest performed at Windlesham, and the next day met Harry for a second lunch, this time in Brighton, and sat among the audience at the Hippodrome for the evening show. Everything he saw reinforced his conviction that, like the Davenport Brothers, Houdini possessed "wonderful powers" and was able to harness a "dematerializing and reconstructing force" that allowed for "the passage of matter through matter." He eventually came to believe that Houdini was "the greatest physical medium of modern times." If only the great magician would recognize the supernatural source of his powers! If only he could be enlisted in the Spiritualist cause! His endorsement would cause a sensation. "My dear chap," Sir Arthur wrote, mildly exasperated with his new friend, "why do you go around the world seeking demonstration of the occult when you are giving one all the time?" But whenever Houdini was asked outright if he benefited from supernatural aid, he denied it. As he told Teddy Roosevelt, his tricks were hocus-pocus.

The combination of Spiritualism's burgeoning popularity, Conan Doyle's celebrity, and the sense that the illustrious author was wooing him was tremendously attractive to Houdini, who became somewhat obsessed with the great man and his sacred cause. He kept a file of press clippings about Conan Doyle, bought souvenirs and merchandise relating to Sherlock Holmes, and went so far as to buy a portfolio of work by Conan Doyle's father, Charles A. Doyle, an illustrator and watercolorist with a visionary streak and a fatal weakness for drink.

Although skeptical by nature and made more so by his profession, Houdini had not yet ruled out the possibility that communication with the dead might somehow be achieved. In their medicine show days he and Bess had dabbled in Spiritualism in a cynical way, and those fraudulent tent-show séances left a sour taste—it was, as he put it, a "Bad effect." He regretted the "crime" of trifling with hopes of the bereaved. Now, seven years after his mother's death, still prone to spells of sorrow, he knew from bitter experience the intensity with which a mourner yearns for contact with the deceased. He wanted to believe in an afterlife, wanted to believe that his mother had joined his father in a "Meeting Place," and yet he'd never seen credible evidence of the dead communicating with the living, and wasn't sure they had any urge to do so. According to Maimonides, the Jewish philosopher prized by Harry's father, the afterlife is where the spirits of the departed receive their just reward— which might well be punishment. Either way, Maimonides believed souls in the afterlife had no physical dimension, no body, no voice. The Torah expressly forbids séances ("Let no one be found among you . . . who is a medium or spiritist or who consults the dead"), but Houdini never felt bound by Jewish law. Although he indulged his longing for his mother, he trusted in his own experience, which taught him that the wall between the living and the dead was impenetrable.

In his dealings with Conan Doyle he continued to mask his skepticism. He did not, for example, publicly challenge the laughable photographic fraud of the Cottingley Fairies, though he knew all about "camera trix" from starring in motion pictures. For the sake of his friendship with a celebrated author he assumed the role of the sympathetic inquirer who would like nothing better than to be convinced. And there was another matter to consider: exposing Spiritualism as a hoax meant disappointing the legion of people like Sir Arthur, some as nice and sweet as he, who genuinely believed that the dead were still among us, eager to commune with the living, waiting to be summoned by a medium.

All sorts of eerie, uncanny things happen during a séance. After the lights are dimmed, while the sitters and the medium hold hands in an unbroken chain, the table is rapped, loudly, or perhaps it tips or levitates. Various participants are touched in unlikely places at unexpected moments. Bizarre or ordinary objects materialize, they fly through the air. Auras appear, glowing bright or flickering suggestively. Music is heard, as well as strange unmusical sounds. The medium speaks in tongues, sometimes through a levitating spirit trumpet (a kind of ghost megaphone). A sticky substance—ectoplasm, it was called—oozes from an orifice in the medium's body. Sometimes the ectoplasm takes the shape of a human visage resembling someone's dead relative. Conan Doyle considered that these occult manifestations, all produced in the dark, were emanations of "the lowest and most mechanical plane of the spiritual world." What he prized was any intelligible message from beyond the grave. If a medium could summon the true voice of the departed, and say something distinctive and personal, then authentic contact had been made, further proof of immortality of the spirit and the proximity of the dead to the living—proof, in short, of the existence of a spirit world. Automatic writing of the kind Lady Conan Doyle produced was similarly valuable, with the added benefit that it produced a tangible record of the spirit's utterance.

What looks laughable from a twenty-first-century perspective seemed plausible a hundred years ago, even to distinguished scientists. A variety of physical phenomena, some recently discovered, some recently harnessed, had transformed daily life and altered our understanding of the universe. Electricity, radio waves, X-rays, gamma rays—all these might be emanations of a spirit world yet to be revealed. Obscure forces were at work, currents of energy running below the surface, or in the ether, out of sight, undetected and as yet inconceivable. Albert Einstein explored the nature of four-dimensional space-time with his theory of general relativity—how soon would a fifth dimension be discovered? Also hidden from view was the psychic energy of the subconscious, what Sigmund Freud called the id. Mysterious elements operated within and without—who could be sure that the occult wasn't one of them? The supernatural might be a dimension of the physical world awaiting scientific discovery.

Houdini's turn of mind was nontheoretical, hands-on, nononsense. He was predisposed to believe that spirit messages were bogus and that psychic manifestations were produced by stagecraft of the sort he practiced for a living. Curious, both intellectually and professionally, and hopeful (thinking not only of his mother but of himself), he assumed that mediums achieved their effects through trickery—sleight of hand and other deceptions—and wanted to know in each case exactly how the scam worked.

Once again on his new friend's recommendation, he attended half a dozen séances with a French medium who called herself Eva C. and was adept at excreting an ooze of ectoplasm. These séances, held on June evenings at the London headquarters of the Society for Psychical Research on Hanover Street, lasted three hours or more and were elaborately and strictly controlled to minimize the possibility that Eva C. might be faking it. Houdini nonetheless concluded that she was a fraud— but tactfully refrained from saying so to Sir Arthur. Instead, he perfected the art of the mildly affirmative waffle: "I have had a wonderful lot of interesting sittings during my stay over here and thoroughly enjoyed them," he wrote before sailing home on July 3, 1920.

Such was the friendly, lighthearted tone of the transatlantic correspondence they maintained before they met again in person nearly two years later, in early April 1922, when Conan Doyle, his wife, and their three children arrived in New York for his evangelical "American Mission." The eleven-week tour consisted of Conan Doyle's lectures on Spiritualism (all sold out); visits with mediums and psychics, whom he inevitably found credible; and sightseeing for the benefit of the children.

The lectures were phenomenally successful. He filled the main auditorium of New York's Carnegie Hall, which seats more than twenty-eight hundred, on four different occasions, and so arranged for three additional performances in the city. His delivery was neither polished nor flamboyant, but he struck listeners as sincere and trustworthy. He explained that a spirit self, or "etheric body," survived death and might be reunited with deceased loved ones; that heaven was very much like earth, with similar creature comforts; and that happiness in the afterlife was the reward of the virtuous. (New York newspapers distilled this hopeful message in such headlines as, "Doyle Says Marital Relations OK in Next World.") The evidence he produced in support of his claims was mostly anecdotal and personal, stories of his encounters with the spirits of departed relatives. He also projected onto a screen spirit photographs, images that purported to show the ghosts of the dead, invisible to the living eye but captured on the photographic plate. There was a photo of himself seated in a chair with his late son Kingsley hovering beside him, and also a notorious photo of a crowd gathered on Armistice Day to commemorate the war dead at the Cenotaph in London; over the crowd, floating in an etheric cloud, were the faces of fallen heroes. (A series of these Cenotaph spirit photos were taken annually on November 11 by a medium called Ada Emma Deane. In 1924 they were exposed as a hoax by a London newspaper that pointed out that some of the faces hovering over the crowd could be identified—not as the valiant war dead but as living athletes, among them a boxer and a footballer.) Sometimes hecklers derided Sir Arthur's claims, but he handled these interruptions with grace and wit, and the vast majority of those who heard him speak were prepared to give him the benefit of the doubt. His own honesty was beyond question; the fact that he trusted spirit mediums and believed in spirit photographs argued in favor of both. Impossible to think that the man who gave us the infallibly perspicacious Sherlock Holmes could be fooled by fraudsters.

Houdini attended one of the Carnegie Hall lectures, and tracked Conan Doyle's progress as he made his way from city to city. The newspapers covered the British author's every move, and Houdini collected, annotated, and filed away a steady flow of press clippings. The two men continued to correspond, and a date was fixed for a lunch at 278.

At eleven o'clock on May 10, 1922, the Houdinis welcomed the Conan Doyles to their Harlem brownstone, along with another guest, Bernard Ernst, who was Houdini's lawyer and a fellow magician. The host showed off his collection of memorabilia (including the bronze bust of himself commissioned for the exedra at the family tomb) and his vast library of Spiritualist material. Harry presented Sir Arthur with a pamphlet one of the Davenport Brothers had given him, and Sir Arthur presented Harry with an inscribed copy of his latest book, *The Wanderings of a Spiritualist.* Over lunch Sir Arthur proposed a toast to friendship. Lady Conan Doyle told Bess that 278 was a "most home-like home."

After the meal the men repaired to the library, where Houdini arranged an elaborate session of spirit writing: cork balls soaked in white ink moving apparently unaided across a slate suspended in the center of the room and writing a message identical to the one Conan Doyle had scribbled unobserved on a piece of paper. Ernst, himself an able conjuror, professed to be amazed by this "experiment," as did Conan Doyle, who insisted that Houdini must have employed "psychic means." Their host assured them that the feat was accomplished "by trickery and nothing else."

It's hard to understand why Houdini would take the trouble to perform for his gullible guest a complex magic trick that required extensive and meticulous preparation. If it was to demonstrate the marvelous things that could be achieved by hocus-pocus and thereby dent Conan Doyle's credulity, Houdini should have dispelled the mystery by exposing his own trickery and explaining the mechanics. Instead, he accompanied his guests back to their hotel, and in the taxi performed another trick, this one so elementary that it's practiced by children all over the world: he pretended, by sleight of hand, to detach and replace the end of his thumb. Sir Arthur and Lady Conan Doyle were stunned, bamboozled afresh by the simplest of illusions.

Was Harry trying to make a fool of his famous friend? His motivation was mixed. His need to perform, to amaze and delight, played its part, as did his desire to cement a valued friendship by entertaining his guests as only he could. But his competitive urge was also at work. He was establishing in his own mind a certain superiority over a literary titan renowned for his intellect. He recorded his judgment on Sir Arthur's credulity

with a hint of smug satisfaction: "Never having been taught the artifices of conjuring, it was the simplest thing in the world to gain his confidence and hoodwink him."

To hoodwink Houdini was, of course, impossible, and yet sadly that's what Lady Conan Doyle attempted several weeks later. The Conan Doyles had taken up residence in a suite at the swank new Ambassador Hotel in Atlantic City, and they invited the Houdinis to "come down" for the weekend. Sir Arthur joked that the children would teach Harry, who had often defied a watery death, how to swim. Bess and Harry accepted and Harry spent much of Saturday afternoon splashing in the hotel pool with the kids and amazing everyone by holding his breath underwater for an impossibly long time. Later on he and Sir Arthur sat on the beach and talked about spirit photography—with great enthusiasm on the author's part—while the children played beach ball nearby.

Harry and Bess were back on the beach on Sunday morning, sitting on deck chairs in the sun, when Sir Arthur appeared and invited Harry—but not Bess, who was politely but firmly excluded—to an automatic-writing séance in which Lady Conan Doyle would try to summon the spirit of Harry's mother. (Bess's presence, she was told, might impede communication with the spirit world. The Conan Doyles wanted to focus their attention on Harry.)

The séance took place at a small round table in the Conan Doyles' darkened suite. Lady Conan Doyle, equipped with pencil and a writing pad, rapped sharply three times with her fist, and marked the first sheet of paper with the sign of the cross. Shortly thereafter she began to scribble furiously, covering page after page with a long message from Cecilia Weiss, dead these nine years. "Oh, my darling, thank God," the scrawled communication read, "at last I'm through—I've tried so often—now I am happy." Her happiness was something Cecilia's spirit insisted upon: the "only shadow has been that my beloved one hasn't known how often I have been with him all the while." But thanks to the Conan Doyles, she finally "bridged the gulf—that is what I wanted, oh so much. Now I can rest in peace." Before signing off, she made sure to express her gratitude to the "friend" facilitating this contact across the gulf, and the friend's husband as well: "God bless you, too, Sir Arthur, for what you are doing for us—for us over here—who so need to get in touch with our beloved ones on the earth plane."

According to Conan Doyle, Houdini was unnerved by the séance: "He sat silent, looking grimmer and paler every moment." Cecilia's spirit had urged him to attempt automatic writing himself ("Tell him I want him to try to write at his own home"). Asking about the proper technique, he picked up a pencil and wrote the name "Powell." Conan Doyle pounced on this as proof that Houdini was possessed of occult powers: "The spirits have directed you in writing the name of my dear fighting partner in Spiritualism, Dr. Ellis Powell, who has just died in England." Elated, Sir Arthur declared Houdini a medium: "Truly Saul is among the prophets." Houdini replied that he was thinking about a man named Frederick Eugene Powell. (This Powell was a magician poised to help promote *The Man from Beyond*, which had a pronounced Spiritualist slant.) He then gathered up the fifteen pages of scrawled writing and hurried out the door.

None of the accounts of the séance is entirely reliable. Houdini took some notes a few hours after leaving the suite, and wrote and talked about the events of that Sunday for years to come. He even produced a notarized "deposition" in which he placed his version "on record" for posterity. Conan Doyle, too, wrote frequently about the Atlantic City incident. They contradicted themselves and each other, especially concerning Houdini's state of mind as he watched Lady Conan Doyle transcribe a message that she insisted came from his beloved mother. "I had made up my mind that I would be as religious as it was in my power to be," Houdini claimed, "and not at any time did I scoff at the ceremony. I excluded all earthly thoughts and gave my whole soul to the séance." He was "waiting for a sign or vibrations, feeling for the presence of my dearly beloved Mother." He was especially keen to contact her, he explained, because it was her birthday. (In fact Cecilia had been born on June 17, which was the day before.) But he also claimed that Bess had revealed to him that she had told Lady Conan Doyle the night before the séance of his great love for his mother— and that therefore he had entered the Conan Doyles' suite expecting that "some business was about to occur." He would have us believe that he was hopeful and receptive ("I was *willing* to believe, even *wanted* to believe") and at the same time wary and suspicious.

Sir Arthur variously claimed that the séance was his idea ("a sudden inspiration of mine") and that it was Houdini's ("at his own urgent request and against my wife's desire"). He reported that when he saw Houdini two days later in New York, Harry gave him the impression that he was "profoundly moved" by the experience and admitted that he had been "walking on air ever since." For his part, Houdini insisted that he never put any faith in the authenticity of the communication dictated to Lady Conan Doyle: it was in English, a language Cecilia never learned to speak (or read or write), it was written under the sign of the cross (not congenial to a rabbi's wife), and it contained no specifics about the relationship between mother and son. In other words, he was looking pale and grim during the séance because he was annoyed and offended. It's also possible that rising anger rather than a spirit guide or mere coincidence moved him to write the name Powell. It would be just like Houdini to have discovered that Conan Doyle's fellow Spiritualist had died and to put that knowledge to work in a needling, provocative way. He could have predicted with absolute certainty the consequence of his one-word foray into automatic writing.

The séance was the wedge that would eventually pry them apart and fracture their friendship, but at first Houdini went on dissembling, keeping his doubts to himself. "I did not have the nerve to tell him," he later explained. He was coming around to the idea that the Conan Doyles suffered from "religious mania," that they truly believed that those fifteen scrawled pages were the genuine article: neither husband nor wife was *conscious* of trying to hoodwink him.

And so they remained friends. The Conan Doyles attended a New York screening of *The Man from Beyond* and expressed their delight at the cameo role played in the final scene by Conan Doyle's *The New Revelation*—product placement guaranteed to tickle any author. And the tickled author returned the favor by providing an endorsement of the film: "The very best sensational picture I have ever seen," he blurbed. "It holds one breathless." On June 23, when the Conan Doyle family set sail for England, Houdini escorted them to the pier, snapped farewell photos on the deck of the RMS *Adriatic*, told the assembled reporters of the "admiration, fondness and respect" he felt for Sir Arthur, and made sure that a bon-voyage bouquet was waiting in the great man's cabin.

Exactly a week later, Houdini sent to the *New York Times* a letter that is a masterpiece of equivocation. Privately skeptical about all aspects of Spiritualism, in public, and for the benefit of Sir Arthur, Houdini was sitting uncomfortably on the fence. "I have one of the largest libraries of the world on psychic and spiritualistic data, have personally met all the great clairvoyants and am yet open to be convinced. I want to put on record that I do not say there is no such thing as Spiritualism, but state that in the thirty years of my investigation nothing has caused me to change my mind."

Posing as an agnostic was clearly a struggle. In late October, in an article in the *New York Sun*—the duration of his "investigation" now trimmed by five years—he made a seemingly straightforward declaration: "In the twenty-five years of my investigation and the hundreds of séances which I have attended, I have never seen or heard anything that could convince me that there is a possibility of communication with the loved ones who have gone beyond." Yet in the same breath he assured the reader, "I am not a skeptic regarding Spiritualism," and promised, "My mind is open. I am perfectly willing to believe."

Conan Doyle expressed disappointment in a letter dated November 19, 1922. The implication of the *Sun* article was that the Atlantic City séance was a sham, which was an affront to his wife. "I felt rather sore about it," Sir Arthur admitted. "I know by many examples the purity of my wife's mediumship, and I saw what you got and what the effect was upon you at the time." Houdini wrote back, explaining once again why he couldn't bring himself to believe that the message dictated to Lady Conan Doyle was genuinely from his mother. He added that he held both Sir Arthur and Lady Conan Doyle "in the highest esteem."

More trouble was brewing. *Scientific American*, a magazine

highly respected since its founding in 1845, announced two cash prizes of $2,500 each to anyone who could provide "conclusive psychic manifestations." One prize was offered for a spirit photograph produced under "the fullest and most objective scrutiny," and the other for "visible occult manifestations" produced at a séance. Seeking a "scientific basis" for judging supernatural effects, the magazine established strict guidelines for the contest and appointed a committee of five judges, one of whom was Harry Houdini. His new colleagues were all either academics or writers, and one of them was chairman of the department of psychology at Harvard, which gave Harry a pretext for labeling them the "learned professors." Although delighted to find himself in such erudite company, he worried that these rarefied intellectuals could be quite easily fooled.

News of his appointment displeased Sir Arthur. "I see that you are on the *Scientific American* committee," he wrote in January 1923. Noting that Houdini had announced his skepticism in the press, he added, "You have every possible right to hold such an opinion, but you can't sit on an impartial committee afterwards. It becomes biased at once." Although in the same letter he generously held out hope for a positive outcome ("it may work out all right"), he was being polite. In truth he believed that the magazine had blundered badly by appointing Houdini and that the committee, as a result, was a "farce."

Newspapers all over America reported on every twist and turn of "The Great Spirit Hunt," and from the beginning the consensus was that the hardheaded Houdini was just the man to conduct a rigorous investigation. He and Conan Doyle began sparring in the pages of the *New York Times*, and by the time the British author landed in New York for another U.S. tour (dubbed by one witty reporter "The Second Coming of Sir Arthur"), the press had decided that the two friends were now antagonists locked in a protracted duel over the legitimacy of Spiritualism. On March 28, 1923, on the eve of Conan Doyle's arrival, a *New York Mail* headline reveled in the prospect of a celebrity dust-up: "Sir Arthur Coming to Answer Houdini!"

In fact, Houdini was himself on tour when the Conan Doyles disembarked, and Sir Arthur paused only briefly in New York City before making his way to the West Coast, once again with wife and children in tow. It wasn't until early May, at the venerable Brown Palace Hotel in Denver, that their paths crossed. They greeted each other with friendly courtesy, pretending their disagreements were solely the invention of scandal-mongering journalists. The two families had lunch together at the hotel, publicly contradicting the alliterative headline in the *Morning Express:* "Doyle in Denver Defies Houdini." Doyle apologized for the article, saying that his remarks had been grossly misrepresented. Houdini agreed that "frequently the papers misquote people." The two men took a drive together in the scenic outskirts of Denver, they sat together in a park—but the topic, inevitably, was Spiritualism, about which they were bound to disagree.

Sir Arthur went to see Houdini's show at Denver's vast Orpheum Theatre. Bess attended Sir Arthur's lecture at the slightly smaller Ogden Theatre; later she assured her husband that his was the more "interesting and convincing" performance. In his diary Harry made a note of his reply to her: "Doyle is a historical character and his word goes far, in fact much further than mine." Recognizing that truth may have brought about a change in attitude: less than two weeks later, in Oakland, Houdini turned up the volume when talking about Conan Doyle to a reporter from the *Oakland Tribune:* he explained that the "distinguished Britisher" had been repeatedly duped by discredited mediums. The article appeared under the ominous headline: "Houdini Unmasks the Mediums." Conan Doyle, who was by now in Los Angeles, received the message loud and clear and sent off a flurry of angry letters demanding a retraction. "I must really ask you to deny over your signature [the] really injurious statements you have made. . . . I am very sorry this breach has come, as we have felt very friendly towards Mrs Houdini and yourself, but 'friendly is as friendly does,' and this is not friendly, but on the contrary it is outrageous to make such arguments with no atom of truth in them."

This time the breach was irreparable. Although Houdini had returned to New York in early August when the Conan Doyle family sailed for England, there were no fond shipboard farewells, no photos, no flowers. It was back in Denver, when they were smiling through gritted teeth in the lofty atrium of the Brown Palace Hotel, that the two men saw each other for the last time.

* * *

In the summer of 1923 Houdini deliberately set himself up as an anti–Conan Doyle: he began giving talks about Spiritualism at universities, mostly in the Midwest. In his diary he wrote, "Wait till Sir A.C. Doyle hears of my lectures! Whew!!!" In February 1924, he signed with the Coit-Alber Lyceum Bureau to speak in twenty-four venues across the country. The first stop of the tour, where he lectured on "Fraudulent Spiritualistic Phenomena," was the Plaza Hotel in Boston.

Although he would not have described the debunking of Spiritualism and the unmasking of bogus mediums as a sacred cause, it was certainly a crusade. "I do believe it is my duty, for the betterment of humanity, to place frankly before the public the results of my long investigation into Spiritualism," he wrote in *A Magician among the Spirits*, published in May. This was the book he'd begun thinking about four years earlier, after his lunch with Conan Doyle at Windlesham Manor. Variously presented as the fruit of "twenty-five years of ardent research and endeavor" and as an "investigation . . . that has extended over thirty years," it was part manifesto, part condensed history, part how-to manual—another hodgepodge, again written with the aid of a ghostwriter, this time his private secretary and research assistant, Oscar Teale. Houdini was proud of the book, which was reviewed extensively and for the most part favorably, though when it was justly criticized for factual errors and misattributions, he blamed the publisher, Harper & Brothers, claiming that the press had rushed him and "mutilated" the text, cutting a hundred thousand words from the manuscript he'd submitted—an exaggeration, as usual.

Harry sent a copy of *A Magician among the Spirits* to Sir Arthur, but his letter went unanswered, hardly surprising given the battering he gave the poor man. "I have no desire to discredit Spiritualism," he wrote. "I have no warfare with Sir Arthur; I have no fight with the Spiritists." But in fact he did his level best to discredit the notion that communication with the dead was possible, waged an implacable war of words on his former friend, and attacked mediums of all stripes, exposing their methods and condemning their dishonesty.

The book advanced his claim to being the world's preeminent psychic investigator, and dovetailed with the lectures. These were illustrated by a series of lantern slides, including photographs of the principal actors in the history of Spiritualism, from the Fox sisters to Arthur Conan Doyle. Still more slides showed ectoplasm, paraffin spirit hands, and levitating objects—the special effects he proceeded to debunk. He warmed up his audience with a brief account of his own career as a medium, the old days of the "Bad effect," touring the Midwest with Dr. Hill's medicine show. Lasting about ninety minutes, with the occasional magic trick stirred in to add spice, the talks were a hit.

He liked being recognized as an expert, a trusted authority on Spiritualism and the occult, a "psychic Diogenes," as one newspaper called him. He liked the idea that he was an educator as well as an entertainer, and that he was beating Sir Arthur at his own game. He liked the tremendous publicity generated every time he disparaged a medium or sabotaged a séance. And he also relished a good fight. He admitted in private what he denied in public: in both his book and his lectures he was doing battle with Spiritualists.

Writing several years after Houdini's death, Conan Doyle argued that it was his "desire to play a constant public part which had a great deal to do with his furious campaign against Spiritualism. He knew that the public took a keen interest in the matter, and that there was unlimited publicity to be had from it." True enough, but there was more to it than that. Some part of Harry's fury came from dashed hopes. His investigations into spirit phenomena were colored by grief and longing for his dead mother, and when the inevitable fakery was exposed he was angry and dejected. Cecilia would not speak to him from beyond the grave, and every exposed fraudster and cheap occult trick made that sad fact more apparent. Fakery demeaned mourning—and mourning, to Harry, was sacred.

There was another element to his campaign: professional pride. The mediums he unmasked gave magic a bad name: he exposed them as shoddy, second-rate illusionists. Anything they could do, he could do better. And what he did, he did by himself, with his wit, his dexterity, his strength, his endurance— without any supernatural assistance. His was a skill—an art, perhaps—which he'd perfected through years of rigorous and patient training. But here in these gloomy séance chambers were these . . . *amateurs* . . . putting on poor shows (in the dark!) and not even taking responsibility for the success of their illusions. It was always spirit manifestation—a clever ghost—never the ingenuity of the medium. The whole scene was tawdry, and tawdry was exactly what Houdini's worldwide success allowed him to avoid.

Launching himself into this new phase of his career with the usual gusto, he crisscrossed the country, rarely spending more than a night in the same town, a punishing schedule—a "hard grind," he called it. In addition to the lectures, he talked on the radio and at civic clubs, presented his vaudeville act of escapes and magic, and performed suspended straitjacket escapes in most of the cities he visited. And all the while he was busy exposing mediums as charlatans—or rather investigating psychic phenomena that were sooner or later revealed to be shabby tricks.

A parade of professional mediums put themselves forward in the eighteen months after *Scientific American* announced its prize, and all were dismissed with relatively little fuss. First up was George Valiantine, a tubby Pennsylvanian rube who claimed to be in touch with a Native American spirit guide named Kokum. Valiantine caused spirit trumpets to fly around the room and spoke in gibberish, and in languages he claimed not to know. Houdini, who dubbed him "the jolly medium," telephoned the *New York Times* a few days after the final sitting in the library of the *Scientific American* offices in Manhattan's Woolworth Building and gave a lively account of the proceedings:

> The man came there to win the . . . prize, and we agreed to act like a lot of boobs to see what his game was. . . .
>
> The chairs of the judges were arranged in a circle with the chairs of the medium and his assistant in the middle of the circle. The chairs in which the medium and his assistant sat were rigged with electrical contacts, so that when the medium got out of his chair contacts were established and excited an electric light in the next room. . . .
>
> While the séance was in progress the test lights in the adjoining room repeatedly came up, proving that the medium had left his chair—for instance, probably at the moment when Dr. Munn of *The Scientific American* was whacked on the nose by the end of the trumpet and lost his glasses. . . .
>
> There wasn't a chance at any time that this magician fooled us. I think those people ought to be put in jail for preying on the most sacred of human emotions.

Besides offering us a chance to hear Houdini's voice transcribed ("Gee, I got an awful clout on the head"), the report in the *Times* is further evidence, if any were needed, of his wild craving for publicity. *Scientific American*, and especially associate editor J. Malcolm Bird (secretary of the committee, a nonvoting role), had asked that no results of the test be revealed without the authorization of the magazine. No authorization was forthcoming, and yet Houdini picked up the phone and regaled a reporter with every last detail of the séance. J. Malcolm Bird was livid. "And please say," Bird told the *Times* after grudgingly corroborating Houdini's account, "that Mr. Houdini is through right now as a member of that committee and make it plain that he is through because he has violated that understanding."

In fact Houdini's activity as a member of the committee had only just begun. The battle lines were now drawn between him and Bird, and it promised to be a long and vicious fight.

In mid-December, while Houdini was performing at the Majestic Theater in Little Rock, Arkansas, a telegram from Orson Munn, publisher of *Scientific American*, summoned him to New York to test another medium, Nino Pecoraro, aka "the Boy Medium." Pecoraro was a twenty-four-year-old from Naples who channeled the feisty spirit of a famous Italian psychic, Eusapia Palladino, who had died in 1918. Pecoraro's séances resembled the Davenports'. Though securely bound inside a cabinet, he (or the ghost of Palladino) caused objects to fly about— clothing, dollar bills—and musical instruments to sound. In a trance, he spoke in the hoarse voice of Palladino. Some members of the committee were impressed, reports in the press were favorable, but Munn felt Houdini should be consulted—hence the telegram to Little Rock.

Houdini knew exactly what to do with the Boy Medium: bind him so that no one, perhaps not even Houdini, could escape. He explained that only short lengths of rope should be used: the more length, the more slack. It took him an hour and a half to truss up the Italian to his satisfaction, and then, when the lights were dimmed, all the medium could produce was the raspy voice of his spirit guide, a wail of defeat.

Pecoraro and Valiantine were mere warm-up acts for a medium Houdini encountered for the first time in late July 1924: the lithe and lovely Mina Crandon, who called herself "Margery" in the séance room and was known in the press, once the story broke, as the "Blonde Witch of Lime Street." Margery was a formidable candidate who captured the public imagination, galvanized a fanatical group of supporters, and often seemed on the verge of claiming the $2,500 prize. Recognizing her as a resourceful and cunning opponent, Houdini campaigned long and hard to deny her the award and prove that she was, like the others, a fraud.

Born Mina Stinson in Picton, Ontario, in 1889, she moved to Boston as a young woman and married a grocer named Earl Rand. They had one son, Alan. In 1917, after seven years of marriage, Mina was admitted to the Dorchester Hospital with suspected appendicitis. The surgeon who operated on her was Dr. Le Roi Goddard Crandon, a wealthy Harvard-educated Bostonian with a yacht, a cabin in Maine, and a fine house on Beacon Hill. Mina successfully sued Rand for divorce, citing cruelty, and became the third Mrs. Crandon in the fall of 1918. (Dr. Crandon's first two marriages, both brief, ended in divorce.) Having scaled so many rungs of the social ladder in the wink of an eye, Mina and her son settled comfortably in her new husband's four-story brick townhouse at 10 Lime Street, three tree-lined blocks from Boston's Public Garden. The Crandons lived well, looked after by their Japanese butler, Noguchi.

In 1920, having heard a lecture by the eminent British physicist Sir Oliver Lodge (who claimed to be in communication with a son killed early on in the Great War), Dr. Crandon developed an interest in Spiritualism. After corresponding with other scientists and academics, he declared himself "intellectually convinced" that there was life beyond the grave. He became interested in séance experiments, and in the spring of 1923 arranged to try "table-tilting" on the top floor of his Lime Street house, where the library was lit for the occasion with a red lantern and equipped with a specially constructed table, rough-hewn and weighing seventeen pounds. When the Crandons linked hands around the table with the four guests invited to the séance, at first nothing happened. Then the table began to vibrate beneath their hands, to tilt, rise up, crash down. Dr. Crandon asked each of the sitters in turn to leave the room, to see if the table's movement was the work of a particular medium or a phenomenon caused by the assembled group. Only when his wife left the room did the manifestations cease—this was the moment when Mina Crandon's mediumistic talents were discovered.

All summer long the Crandons held séances in their fourth-floor library, and Mina's powers developed apace. Soon she was channeling the voice of her older brother, Walter, who had died in a railroad accident in 1911. A reporter for the *Boston Herald* described the ghost's persona as "vivid, sharply defined and unforgettable. His moods are swift and evanescent. By turns he is gay, impudent, ironic, ribald, but always witty, with a gamin-like ability for a quick retort or a cutting phrase." He spouted limericks, this wisecracking spirit. Walter could whisper in a sitter's ear or move about the darkened, red-lit room, his teasing voice emanating from one corner or another. He could whistle, too, which Mina claimed she could not. Adept at levitating the séance table, he could move it around to the rhythm of the foxtrot playing on the Victrola. In late November he caused a live dove to appear and perch on the edge of the table. In the spring he specialized in making objects move around the room: anything left on the table was sure to scoot about or levitate or become a projectile. Spirit lights began to flash, bright pulsing displays in various shapes and colors that foretold the eventual emanation of some ectoplasmic form.

Mina was in almost every respect an unusual medium. She had nothing to gain by conducting séances: she was clearly not after anyone's money, and she insisted that she had no desire to convert anyone to Spiritualism. She shied away from publicity, and professed to be alternately baffled and amused by the effects she produced. Polished and plausible and very pretty, she had bright eyes, a shapely figure, and a flapper's blond bob. She was, in a word, disarming.

Within weeks of her first séance, she attracted the attention of the Harvard psychology department. Two professors, one of them Dr. William McDougall, who was both chairman of the department and president of the American Society for Psychical Research (ASPR), began visiting Lime Street, hoping to find a natural (nonsupernatural) explanation for the bizarre goings-on in the Crandons' library. Dr. McDougall was one of the "learned professors" on the committee of the *Scientific American* prize. The Harvard duo investigated for months and remained baffled, unable to find evidence of fraud.

Mina also attracted the attention of Houdini's antagonist J. Malcolm Bird, who visited Lime Street in mid-November. The next month the Crandons crossed the Atlantic to meet the most eminent European psychic investigators. Mina wowed them in Paris and wowed them in London. Arthur Conan Doyle, to whom Dr. Crandon had written seeking advice on how best to nurture his wife's occult talent, invited the Crandons to meet him in the lobby of the Grosvenor Hotel, next to Victoria Station. After a spectacular séance in his suite, Sir Arthur became Mina's ardent champion. He declared her to be "a very powerful medium" whose authenticity was "beyond all question." He deemed her an excellent prospect for the *Scientific American* contest and urged her to enter.

By the time Bird made his second visit to Lime Street, in April 1924, Mina had agreed to be tested by the committee—but only under certain conditions. The Crandons didn't want their name in the papers, so Bird suggested she adopt Margery as her *nom de séance*. And the preliminary tests, at least, were to take place where Margery felt most at home, on the top floor of the house. The Crandons were prepared to cover the cost of bringing the committee up to Boston, so in essence the members of the committee were to be Margery's guests while they weighed the authenticity of her powers. The tests were to be performed in stages, with the full committee eventually gathering to assess her only if no natural explanation for the psychic phenomena could be found along the way. Bird camped out at the Crandons' house for much of the summer, with séances held night after night, and he grew more and more convinced that Margery was a genuine spirit medium. He was also seduced by her charm, and so became lodger, investigator, and admirer.

Bird was by no means the only investigator at Lime Street that summer. Professors of psychology and professors of physics rubbed elbows with conjurors and full-time spook hunters. Some, such as Hereward Carrington, the British-born founder of the American Psychical Institute, a yoga fanatic and a vegetarian, were judges on the *Scientific American* committee; some were not. At least one—the tall, gaunt, handsome Carrington—became Mina Crandon's lover. Several others, including Bird, wished they were.

In July, Bird went public with his preliminary judgment in an enthusiastic summary of the séances for *Scientific American*, which in turn sparked sensational stories in the press. "'Margery' Passes All Psychic Tests," blared the *New York Times* on July 22, 1924.

Infuriated by Bird's article, and convinced that Bird was trying to award the prize behind his back, Houdini took the train to Boston on July 23 to join the Lime Street circus. He was accompanied by Oscar Munn, who was concerned that Houdini would charge like a buffalo into the Beacon Hill household. As Bird put it, Margery was "a lady of refinement and culture"— Houdini mustn't stampede her.

Margery may have been refined and cultured, but Walter wasn't. At a séance the night before Houdini's arrival, he spouted a little ditty:

> Harry Houdini, he sure is a sheeney,
> A man with a crook in his shoe.
> Says he, "As to Walter,
> I'll lead him to slaughter."
> "But," says Walter, "Perhaps I'll get you!"

When Margery greeted Houdini at 10 Lime Street, there was no antagonism on either side, no anti-Semitic slurs, no furious, skeptical impatience. Harry was politely inquisitive and friendly; Mrs. Crandon was welcoming and gracious. She gave her guest a tour of the neighborhood. At dinner they sized each other up. Harry was impressed with the good taste of the furnishings and the beauty of the hostess. She found him dignified. Her husband showed off his collection of Lincoln memorabilia, which allowed Houdini to boast about his theater collection, particularly the items relating to the actor John Wilkes Booth, Lincoln's assassin.

The first séance passed without a hitch. Walter spoke, lights flashed, bells rang, a trumpet flew through the air—Houdini signed a report acknowledging that he had witnessed these phenomena.

After the séance Bird, who was as usual the Crandons' houseguest, drove Munn and Houdini to the Copley Plaza Hotel, where the two men were staying. On Beacon Street he pulled over and parked so that they could conduct an impromptu "post mortem" in the car. The illusionist didn't hesitate to declare Margery a charlatan. "Well, gentleman," he announced, "I've got her. All fraud—every bit of it. One more sitting and I will be ready to expose everything." He explained how Margery stretched her foot to ring the bell, how she balanced the trumpet on her head before making a jerking motion to cause the trumpet to fly. Munn asked how the medium had caused the Victrola to stop playing. Houdini believed that a confederate had done it—that there were two cheats in the séance room. Bird was his prime suspect.

The next day Margery made no secret of the fact that she was aware of everything that had been said during the postmortem, which only confirmed Houdini's suspicions: her houseguest had clearly filled her in. That evening's séance was held at the Charlesgate Hotel, a gloomy turreted pile at the far end of Beacon Street, in the apartment of a committee member, Dr. Daniel Comstock. This test was more strictly controlled. It began with a strip search of Margery's person, conducted by Comstock's female secretary. An MIT physicist, Dr. Comstock was well organized and meticulous. He had designed most of the apparatus used to test the medium. But again it was Houdini who detected the fraud, this time discovering that to tilt and overturn the table Margery stretched forward and down and stuck her head underneath it. When the magician caught her in that posture, the medium explained that she was looking for a dropped hairpin.

Conferring in the next room, Houdini and his colleagues had a brief, sharp disagreement about whether to expose Margery at once with a telephone call to a major newspaper. Bird argued that the full committee should meet to test the medium and issue an official report. Uncharacteristically, Houdini backed down.

He and Munn took the midnight train back to New York. During the journey, Houdini wrote an entry in his diary: "Bird is a *traitor*. . . . He must have helped her at seances. He is very intimate with her." He pushed that line of attack with Munn over the next few weeks and gradually undermined the publisher's confidence in his editor.

In the press, the *Scientific American* contest had become a duel between the escape artist and the witch of Lime Street. "Margery to Rassle with the Handcuff King" promised one headline. The *Boston Herald* reported, "Four out of the five men selected as jury are thoroughly convinced that the Boston woman is 100 percent genuine, and it is believed that announcement of the award will come within a few days." The identity of the skeptical fifth man was no secret, though he'd refrained from adding to the media frenzy by making public his firm conviction that the Boston woman was 100 percent fraud.

By the time the committee met again, for three séances in the last week in August, Bird had been sidelined and a new method had been devised to restrict Margery's movements: she was confined in a specially constructed black wooden cabinet that came to be known as "Houdini's box": with its lid closed, only the medium's head and arms protruded.

All these August séances were held in Comstock's Charlesgate apartment. The first, on Monday the 25th, was fractious from the beginning, then settled into tight-lipped acrimony after it was discovered that a rubber eraser was jamming the bell Margery was meant to ring using her psychic powers. Though no accusations of sabotage were leveled at him, Houdini felt he was under suspicion.

The next night a carpenter's folding ruler (perfect for activating a bell placed out of reach) was found in the cabinet, and this time the accusations were loud, accompanied by furious invective in Walter's hoarse whisper: "Houdini, you goddamn son of a bitch. Get the hell out of here and never come back. . . . What did you do that for, Houdini? You're a bastard for putting up a plant like that on a girl. There is a ruler in that cabinet." The spirit ranted on in a frightening vein: "You won't live forever, Houdini, you've got to die. I put a curse on you now that will follow you every day until you die. And then you'll know better." Needless to say, the rest of the séance was blank.

Did Houdini (or his assistant, Jim Collins, who constructed the box) place the ruler in the cabinet? Was he indeed "putting up a plant" on Margery? Or did Margery smuggle it in to cheat? Or to discredit Houdini by making *him* look like a cheat? Neither the magician nor the medium had any qualms about resorting to subterfuge.

Trying unsuccessfully to keep up an appearance of bonhomie, members of the committee dined with the Crandons at a restaurant outside Boston before the final séance on Wednesday. Houdini claimed that over supper Margery warned him not to expose her in the performances he was scheduled to give at Boston's Keith's Theater in early September. She explained that she didn't want her twelve-year-old son to hear she'd been denounced as a fraud, to which he replied, "Then don't be a fraud." She shot back, "If you misrepresent me from the stage at Keith's, some of my friends will come up and give you a good beating." (Hard to imagine Margery making such a threat in a public place; Walter, however, repeatedly predicted that Houdini would be dead within a year.)

The séance that night was again blank, uneventful except that, according to Houdini's claim (again uncorroborated), Dr. Crandon resorted to a form of bribery by offering to make a $10,000 donation to charity if Houdini could bring himself to see the light and embrace Spiritualism.

Although *Scientific American* didn't issue its official report for another six months, by the end of the third evening's blank séance it was clear to all involved that the magazine was not going to declare Margery a true medium possessed of supernatural psychic powers. No prize would be awarded. Spiritualism had lost the chance to win a coveted endorsement, and Houdini had played a key role in shaping the verdict. "Houdini Routs Pet Spook of Science," proclaimed the *New York Mirror*.

Margery refused to give up the fight, as did Houdini. Claims, counterclaims, denunciations, accusations, protestations of righteous indignation—a cacophony of partisan bickering echoed in the columns of newspapers across the country. Mostly through proxies (her husband, Bird, Carrington, Conan Doyle), though occasionally in her own voice, the medium blasted the magician, who responded in kind and made his clashes with her into a feature of his performances. He reconstructed Houdini's box (with ingenious Houdini alterations, naturally) to demonstrate onstage how it foiled her, and how she attempted to cheat. He also demonstrated what *he* could do while confined in the cabinet (a task made easier by the surreptitious alterations). He published a forty-page pamphlet, *Houdini Exposes the Tricks Used by the Boston Medium "Margery,"* complete with photographs and diagrams, and spent thousands of dollars promoting it. Embroiled in this feud, he managed to alienate, one after another, every member of the *Scientific American* committee. With the bickering spread to the "learned professors," the battle lines, never clear to begin with, blurred past the point of recognition. It was obvious to all involved that Houdini reveled in his newspaper notoriety, that he was behaving like a showman, not a disinterested investigator. "It takes a flimflammer to catch a flimflammer," he crowed in triumph to the *Los Angeles Times*.

For their part, the Crandons rented out Boston's Jordan Hall for what they initially billed as Margery's first public séance, onstage in a vast auditorium. But she thought better of it. Instead, the Crandons sponsored a lecture by a young British psychic researcher, Eric Dingwall, on the wonders of Margery's occult powers. The talk was illustrated with lantern slides and spiced up with vigorous condemnation of Houdini and the

Scientific American. Dingwall's efforts were unavailing. Over the next few years Margery was exposed again and again by a succession of investigators, though she never confessed publicly to fraud and never lost the confidence of her zealous supporters.

Houdini's feud with Margery resembled his feud with Conan Doyle, and there was a similar ambivalence at work in both relationships. Houdini's public, professional attitude toward Margery was purely antagonistic. "A deliberate and conscious fraud," he called her, a hoaxer "whose stock in trade is a bag of tricks." He accused her of being a social climber, and of using her "sex charm" to bamboozle the men tasked with testing her powers. But he admired her resourcefulness and ingenuity (and her lack of scruples!), and wanted to be liked and admired by her. There's some evidence that she did like and admire him—that she, too, was ambivalent. She told a reporter for the *Boston Herald* that she respected Houdini more than any other psychic investigator. "He has both feet on the ground all the time," she said. "At least he's not afraid to say where he stands." Perhaps the most telling illustration of this jumble of emotions is the photograph taken of the two of them on Lime Street near her house on the morning after the first séance—by which time they both already knew that his mind was made up, that he considered her a charlatan and would stop at nothing to expose her. And yet in the photo they're holding hands and looking at each other with more than mere friendliness. They look for all the world like lovers.

They were not (though Houdini later hinted that Margery tried to seduce him). And any fond feelings they secretly harbored were snuffed out by the acrimony of the August Charlesgate séances, the folding ruler fracas, and the shouted curses.

In January 1925 Arthur Conan Doyle wrote a strenuous defense of the Crandons for the *Boston Herald*, an article he hoped would "prick the Houdini bubble forever." Relying on information supplied by Dr. Crandon, he asserted that Houdini "left

Boston a very discredited man" and condemned his "unbalanced judgment." Two days later *Variety* reported that Houdini announced from the stage of the Hippodrome in New York that he'd "notified his attorneys to start an immediate action for slander against Sir Arthur, whom Houdini branded 'a menace to mankind because the public thinks he is just as great a man in the spiritualistic field as he is in writing stories.'" The headline read, "Houdini-Doyle Slander Suit."

No suit was filed, but hostilities between Houdini and the Spiritualists intensified, with newspapers reporting on death threats made against the illusionist. Houdini brushed off these rumors, but was anxious that his demise, should it occur, not be credited to a curse put on him by Walter or any other spirit. Lumping Margery, Dr. Crandon, and their supporters in an apt phrase, he asked a reporter to imagine the jubilant gloating of the "worthy Boston witch-doctors" if by chance he started to cross Fifth Avenue and never made it to the other side.

The worthy Boston witch doctors' animus was tinged with bigotry. In *"Margery" the Medium* (1925), Bird's 518-page account, comically detailed and tediously self-exculpatory, he explained, "Houdini is a Jew, his paternal name being Weiss." Bird added that because of his advanced age ("Houdini is past fifty years old"), he was trying to establish a career less strenuous than his "fatiguing escape tricks"—the implication being that his motivation in adopting the "stage personality of exposer of mediums" was simple greed: he craved publicity and money. The same idea was expressed by the *National Spiritualist*, where Houdini was pointedly referred to as "Mr. Weiss" and identified as "racially a Jew." His crusade was dismissed as "racial bombast." As for his profession: "His Special Sphere is trickery for his own financial gain." The high-minded Dr. Crandon wrote to Conan Doyle to complain about Houdini: "My deep regret is that this low-minded Jew has any claim on the word American." And Conan Doyle himself drifted in the same deplorable direction, stressing that Houdini was "foreign" ("as Oriental," he once put it, "as our own Disraeli"), and always angling for "world-wide advertisement." Noting with dismay that the rest of the *Scientific American* committee hadn't denounced Houdini when he accused Margery of fraud, Sir

Arthur wrote, "Knowing her complete innocence, as they must do, these American gentlemen allowed a man with entirely different standards to make this outrageous attack." Those "different" standards were probably what one of Margery's rich and zealous backers had in mind when he referred to Houdini as a "jew-renegade."

The stench of anti-Semitism was more likely to egg on Houdini than to discourage him. He persisted with his attacks on Margery even as he set out to expand and intensify his broader campaign. "I am waging war," he declared majestically, "on the fraud mediums of this country."

There was a frantic edge to his activity in the first six months of 1925, epitomized by the week in which he commuted between the newly opened Albee Theater, a sumptuous movie palace on Dekalb Avenue in Brooklyn, and the Hippodrome in midtown Manhattan: every evening he was escorted between the two venues, like a high muck-a-muck on a state visit, by policemen on motorcycle. ("Sure an exciting week," he wrote in his diary.) He mixed magic and escapes and anti-Spiritualism on both bills, adding something spectacular if attendance flagged. In the pool at the Hippodrome he escaped—manacled, as always—from a submerged box, an indoor variation on the "Daring Dive" off Battery Park a decade earlier.

On tour again, he devised more elaborate means of exposing spirit frauds. He assembled a team of psychic investigators— "my own secret service department," he called them—who did advance work for him, visiting mediums and laying the groundwork for a public debunking. One of the undercover investigators was Bess; another was her twenty-two-year-old niece, Julia Sawyer, who worked at times as Houdini's onstage assistant. Chief among the "spook spies" was Rose Mackenberg, a talented detective, who would go in disguise to a séance, posing as a grieving wife or mother, or a repressed schoolteacher, and let the medium do his or her worst—which often included unwanted sexual advances. Mackenberg sent detailed reports to Houdini, who would challenge the medium onstage when he came to town—or, more spectacularly, pay a house call.

One of his most dramatic stings came on March 10 at a séance in Cleveland, at the home of a well-established medium called George Renner. Wearing scruffy clothes and thick glasses as his disguise (and accompanied by a local prosecutor and a reporter for the *Cleveland Press*, both incognito), Houdini presented himself as a paying customer. According to the account in the *Press*, Renner showed off some spirit photographs, then switched off the lights and launched into his séance, unaware that under cover of darkness Houdini was sneaking around and coating the spirit trumpets with lampblack. In the midst of a lively demonstration, with the trumpets zipping through the air and sounding loudly, Houdini pulled a flashlight from his pocket and trained it on the startled Renner, whose hands and face were smeared with soot.

"Mr. Renner, you are a fraud," thundered Houdini. "Your hands are full of lampblack. The trumpets are full of lampblack. That's where you got it on your hands."

Renner spluttered, "I have been a medium for forty years and I have never been exposed."

"Well, you are now."

"Who are you?" asked Renner, perspiring.

The triumphant answer: "My name, Mr. Renner, is Houdini."

The medium was charged with obtaining money under false pretenses. Houdini testified at the trial, and Renner was slapped with a $25 fine and a six-month jail sentence. Dozens of others were similarly exposed, prosecuted, and convicted. *I am Houdini! And you are a fraud!*—the threat of those words haunted séance rooms up and down the country. In retaliation, a raft of Spiritualists filed lawsuits accusing him of slander.

Harry had been in a combative mood for some time. Back

in October he had thrown a tantrum when a Los Angeles theater manager made the mistake of supplying the newspapers
with photos of the supporting acts but not the big star. The
diary entry is uncharacteristically contrite: "Lost my temper,"
he wrote. "I raised hell foolishly. . . . All wrong on my part, *but
I could not help it.* I was so sore. I was so sore I had a headache
all that afternoon." On a warm day in July 1925, he was involved in an altercation at the Broadway offices of the Houdina
Radio Control Co., an enterprise founded by an engineer named
Francis P. Houdina. Accompanied by his secretary, Oscar Teale,
Houdini harangued the bewildered owners, complaining that
they were using his name to promote their radio-controlled
automobiles. A fight broke out, furniture was broken, a chan-
delier was smashed, a summons for disorderly conduct was issued, and the newspapers had a field day. (The charges were
dropped when the complainant failed to appear at the hearing.)

* * *

Houdini was unchanged—always unabashedly himself—
but his reputation had evolved impressively in the five years
since his fateful lunch with Arthur Conan Doyle, the encounter that marks the beginning of his anti-Spiritualist campaign.
He was respected as never before. A week after giving a lecture
at the New York Police Academy Detective School ("How to
Catch Fake Spiritualists"), he was the subject of a highly flattering essay in the June 24, 1925, issue of the *New Republic*—a
magazine in which vaudeville acts were rarely discussed. The
author was Edmund Wilson, not yet thirty, not yet the country's most distinguished public intellectual, but already majestically confident in his judgment.

Extravagantly admired in print by a highbrow critic! Vali-
dation of the sweetest kind!

Wilson begins with an appreciation of "one of the most accomplished magicians in the world." He observes that although
Houdini is "a tremendous egoist," he's neither a "smart-aleck"

nor a ham: "When he performs tricks, it is with the directness and simplicity of an expert giving a demonstration." Wilson thinks of him as "an honest earnest craftsman . . . enthusiastic, serious-minded, thoroughgoing and intelligent." He makes note of the distinguishing feature of his career: "Houdini has been most celebrated for his cultivation of the 'escape,' extricating himself from every conceivable kind of strong-box, straitjacket, hand-cuffs and chains under every conceivable kind of circumstances. . . . It is characteristic of Houdini that, not content with the ingenuities of illusion and the perfection of sleight of hand, he should have chosen to excel in that branch of magic which was most dangerous, which took him furthest from the theatre and which offered most opportunity for the untried."

This introduction establishes Houdini's expertise, his daring, and (bizarrely) his honesty. Then comes a pivot to the campaign against Spiritualism and his role in denying Margery the *Scientific American* prize: "The truth is, of course, that in a committee of scientists of which Houdini is a member it is Houdini who is the scientist." Imagine the delight with which the magician read that sentence!

Wilson isn't finished: "Houdini is thus perhaps the first important investigator of spiritualism who is really competent for the task. . . . He has brought to the study of trickery a genuine scientific curiosity: he seems actually now to have become more interested in understanding how effects are produced than in astonishing people with them, and to derive more satisfaction from merely lecturing on the methods of the mediums than in contriving illusions of his own."

More fodder to feed that tremendous ego. With a tidy turn of phrase ("Where he once challenged the world to tie him up, he now challenges it to convince him of the supernatural"), Wilson gets set to proclaim him a hero: "Houdini has appeared at a critical moment in the history of spiritualism and . . . is destined to play an important role in it."

In July, in the *Christian Register*, Houdini showed he was ready and willing to accept a heroic role. Adopting a tone midway between prophet and messiah, he commanded, "Tell the people that all I am trying to do is to save them from being tricked in their grief and sorrows, and to persuade them to leave Spiritualism alone and take up some genuine religion."

No surprise, then, to find him, half a year later, appearing before a congressional committee in Washington, DC. He'd been invited by a New York congressman to give his expert opinion on a bill that would have outlawed fortune-tellers in the District of Columbia. Harry was of course in favor. In his opening statement he declared, "There are only two kinds of medium, those who are mental degenerates and who ought to be under observation, and those who are deliberate cheats and frauds."

The hearings—unorthodox, to say the least—were angry and raucous, the gallery packed with noisy mediums anxious to protect their livelihood. Houdini added to the carnival atmosphere by treating the podium like a vaudeville stage and delivering one of his anti-Spiritualist lectures, complete with demonstrations of séance fakery.

The bill didn't pass—it was never even brought up for a vote—but Harry had had his hour on the political stage. During his testimony he called upon two witnesses: Rose Mackenberg, the chief of his "secret service," and Bess, about whom he said, "Outside of my great mother, Mrs. Houdini has been my greatest friend." Answering yes or no to his comical questioning ("Am I good boy?"), Bess defended his character against the mediums who railed against his perfidy, suggested that he was part of an international Jewish conspiracy, and called him "a pronounced atheist and infidel."

He wasn't an atheist; he wasn't even an agnostic. He certainly wasn't a Christian (though he liked to celebrate Christmas and regularly sent out Christmas cards). He wasn't in league with Jews bent on world domination, or with any other kind of Jew—once he'd been bar mitzvahed he rarely set foot in a synagogue. It's much easier to say what he wasn't than to say what he was, to put a label on his hopeful, skeptical, decidedly undogmatic faith. He believed in a supreme being; he believed in the afterlife. He observed the anniversary of his father's death by reciting Kaddish, the ritual prayer of mourning, wherever he happened to be. Other Hebrew rituals he disregarded or adapted to suit his purposes. Perhaps he should be called a self-liberating American Jew.

Years earlier, in 1918, at the height of his vaudeville fame, he had been interviewed by the show business columnist Louella Parsons for the *New York Morning Telegraph*. She reported that he spoke "in tender, proud tones . . . of his rabbi father, who brought him up in the strict Hebrew church. Houdini is a Jew, and proud of it." Harry told Parsons about meeting Billy Sunday, for twenty years the most popular Christian evangelist in America: "He talked about the Bible to me and I went home and read it; the next day I was a better Jew than I had ever been in my life—that is what Billy Sunday did for me."

9

Sucker Punch

SUCCESS NEVER DIMMED Harry's ambition; it merely whet-
ted his appetite. Over fifty and as busy as ever, he was still
straining for the next triumph. Any attempt to slow him down,
even if self-imposed, was doomed to fail. If anything, the scope
of his ambition widened. He talked of taking a freshman English course at Columbia University, of becoming a professor,
of establishing a University of Magic. He wrote a novel, a romantic detective thriller called *The Zanetti Mystery* (ghostwritten, naturally). He patented a Houdini wind-up toy. He had
lofty plans.

His library and his collections, grown vast and valuable,
occupied more and more of his time. In 1920 he'd hired a full-
time librarian, Alfred Becks, and moved him into a spare bed-
room at 278. Becks, who had spent a decade in charge of the
Harvard theater library, set about the herculean task of indexing
and shelving stacks and stacks of books, pamphlets, theatrical

newspapers, programs, and posters. He calculated that the books alone would take him more than a year to catalogue, even working twelve-hour days. Already in his mid-seventies when he arrived at 278, Becks died in April 1925 of bronchitis. His distraught employer spoke briefly at the funeral; back at home he sat and wept.

Houdini brought to collecting the kind of fierce determination he applied to the development and execution of his escape acts. He had four main categories of interest—magic, Spiritualism, Abraham Lincoln, and drama and theater—but sometimes the urge to acquire led him further afield. He bought, for example, a portable writing desk that belonged to Edgar Allan Poe and a Bible that belonged to Martin Luther. He snapped up autographs of famous Americans whenever he had the chance. The idea that other collectors might own rarer items or that their collections might be more complete drove him to redouble his efforts: he had to have the most, the best, the rarest. He bragged about his magic collection: "If all the libraries in the world were to put all their magical literature under one roof, they would not match mine." As for drama and theater, his stated aim was to own the largest private library in the world. That collection, its value appraised in 1927 at half a million dollars, was sold by the estate after Harry's death and later donated to the University of Texas; it's now in the performing arts collection of the Harry Ransom Center. Houdini had planned to leave his colossal Spiritualism collection to the American Society for Psychical Research, but when the society appointed as its chief research officer the detested J. Malcolm Bird, Houdini amended his will and left it instead to the Library of Congress, which is also where his magic collection went. In all, he bequeathed nearly four thousand books to the Library of Congress.

He had written his will, a convoluted document consisting of twenty-three clauses, during the summer of 1924. In essence, he left one-sixth of the estate and all his household and personal effects to Bess. The rest was to be invested in trust by a New York bank, with the income distributed biannually to Bess and his surviving siblings.

Wills by their nature exert control over the living, and Harry's was particularly meddlesome. To his brother Theodore, aka Dash, aka Hardeen, he left his theatrical effects: the magic tricks and apparatus, including the Water Torture Cell—on the condition that after Dash's death everything be "burnt and destroyed," a final bid to make sure that Houdini's secrets would never be revealed. There was also a proviso on Dash's portion of the trust: he would receive his share only on condition that his "surviving children shall have been confirmed according to Jewish law and tradition (Orthodox or Reformed) or shall be so within three months of my death."

If that last requirement suggests a sudden veneration for the letter of the Jewish law, consider this explicit instruction: "My body is to be embalmed and buried in the same manner in which my beloved mother was buried upon her death." Embalming is a violation of Jewish law—but then so is planting a bust of oneself on one's lavish funeral monument. In both cases, Harry was making sure he would be visible after death, at his wake and at the cemetery.

He was generous with those who had supported him: there were straightforward bequests to his assistants ($500 each) and $1,000 to SAM. And he punished those who had displeased him, notably his sister-in-law, Sadie Weiss (née Glantz). Sadie had been married to Houdini's older brother Nathan, but they divorced in 1917. Ten days later, Sadie married the youngest Weiss brother, Leopold, the radiologist. Harry considered this brother swap a family disgrace and would not forgive it. He went to extraordinary lengths to make sure that Sadie inherited no part of his estate. And he explicitly prohibited Leo from being buried in the family plot.

He asked that his mother's letters to him be tied in a packet and placed under his head in the casket as a cushion. He also asked that a séance be held on the anniversary of his death, in case he was wrong and the spirits of the dead do wish to communicate with the living. He provided Bess with a secret code so that she could be sure it was him making contact and not some fraudulent medium's hocus-pocus. (After his death she held séances every year for a decade: nothing came through and she sensibly decreed that there would be no further attempts.)

The threats of the Spiritualists, their dire predictions of his imminent demise, were clearly preying on him when he drew up his will. But he was used to mortal peril. A death threat is perhaps less than totally terrifying to a man who spends his time leaping off bridges with his hands and feet fettered. It's maybe less scary to have your doom foretold by a pack of charlatans than to be locked in the Torture Cell, upside down and underwater.

* * *

At the end of August 1925, at the Maryland Theater in Baltimore, he fulfilled a long-standing ambition by staging a full evening show with no supporting act. When the new show, simply called *HOUDINI* and advertised as "3 Shows in One," opened in New York in late December, it was not at a vaudeville palace like the Hippodrome but rather at the stately Shubert Theater on 44th Street. (The inaugural production at the Shubert, when it opened in 1913, had been Shakespeare's *Hamlet*, starring the eminent Victorian actor Johnston Forbes-Robertson on his farewell tour of America.) This was a venue steeped in theater history—and here was "Dime Museum Harry," packing the house and holding the stage for a full two and a half hours.

Act 1, "Magic," was yet another attempt to claim the mantle of Master Magician. A throwback to the Grand Magical Revue launched in England eleven years earlier, "Magic" featured Robert-Houdin's Crystal Casket, comely female assistants who were made to vanish then reappear, an attractive assistant who was dismembered then reassembled, yards of silk, bunnies, birds, goldfish, and more than a dozen large-scale mechanical effects. All this conjuring and stage magic was done at a break-neck pace—he "jammed one and a half hours of performance," he admitted, "into an hour"—and accompanied by a glib mono-logue. In act 2, "Houdini Himself, in Person," he showed off the escape acts that had made him famous, Metamorphosis and the Water Torture Cell, and his old needle-swallowing trick. Act 3, "Do the Dead Come Back?" was the greatest hits of his anti-Spiritualism campaign, a condensed amalgam of the lec-ture and the medium-busting routine.

Mastering the logistics of touring with this extravaganza was in itself a mighty feat. The apparatus was transported in a sixty-foot railroad car up and down the East Coast and as far west as Chicago, along with a small army of backstage staff. The vast expense was justified by the box office receipts. As usual, Houdini declared that this was his most successful tour, "fi-nancially and artistically." Reviewers pronounced the escapes "thrilling" and the third act "riveting, like a perverse sort of re-vival meeting." Enthusiasm for the first act was more muted.

An eleven-year-old Orson Welles was taken by his father to see the show during its eight-week run at Chicago's Princess Theatre. The magic, he remembered, was "awful stuff." He had a vivid recollection of a "squat little man in evening clothes": "The first thing he did was march to the front of the stage and rip off his sleeves; he pulled them right off, showing his bare arms. Can you imagine? A short-sleeved tailcoat? Even as a kid, I realized the coarseness of it. It was supposed to be a sort of 'nothing up my sleeve' thing. Then, of course, he proceeded to perform a bunch of silly mechanical tricks that couldn't have involved his sleeves at all." (Welles also claimed that his father took him backstage to meet Houdini. When young Orson showed off a handkerchief trick, Houdini praised his skill but told him, "You must practice a trick, Orson, a thousand times before you perform it.")

The tour ended in May 1926. Several weeks later Hereward Carrington turned up in New York with a handsome young man, probably Italian, who professed to be an Egyptian fakir by the name of Rahman Bey. Performing on Broadway at the Selwyn Theater, Bey demonstrated his "miraculous" control over his own physiological functions—mind over body—including insensibility to pain: he stuck steel needles in his cheeks, skewers into his chest, and so on. The suave Carrington, master of ceremonies, delivered a running commentary, a learned disquisition on the wonders of fakirism. One of Bey's tricks, which strayed uncomfortably close to what Houdini saw as his sacred turf, involved being buried alive in a coffin under a heap of sand. Carrington explained that the fakir put himself into a cataleptic trance, stopping his pulse and respiration entirely.

Houdini, being Houdini, had to prove that he could outlast Bey in any sealed container—without recourse to any cataleptic mumbo jumbo—and so embarked on a three-week training program to prepare himself to meet the challenge. His method can be boiled down to a brief sentence, one that he wrote to a friend afterward: "You simply lie down in a coffin and breathe quietly." That's how he claimed to have accomplished the extraordinary feat performed in August 1926 at the indoor swimming pool of the Shelton Towers Hotel in Manhattan. Sealed inside a galvanized iron casket (wired with an alarm and a telephone), he was lowered into the shallow end of the pool. Eight assistants in swimsuits stood on the coffin to make sure it stayed submerged. Supine in the coffin, eyes wide in the dark, breathing quietly with the calm that comes from complete confidence, he lasted an hour and thirty-one minutes—emerging "deathly white," according to one witness. Although he felt a little weak, and noted a metallic taste in his mouth, he was otherwise unaffected. "Houdini Wins Test in a Sealed Casket," read the headline in the *Times*, "Beats Hindoo's Record."

Pleased with this success, he dreamed up an audacious escape—from inside a giant block of ice, in full view of the audience—but never developed the idea into a workable act. He had a bronze casket made for him by the Boyertown Burial Casket Company. The $2,500 coffin (a few hundred dollars more expensive than the top-of-the-line 1926 Studebaker) was the one he planned to be buried in—but not just yet. In the meantime, he would use it for publicity on his next tour, which was scheduled for the fall. He had conceived of a new stunt: "Buried Alive! Egyptian Fakirs Outdone"—only in this case the idea was to escape rather than to lie down and breathe quietly. A casket was placed in a glass-fronted vault; Houdini climbed in (manacled), and the audience watched as a ton of sand was poured on top, burying the coffin and the magician. Two minutes later he was out again—outdoing every last fakir, Egyptian or Hindoo.

The second tour, a five-month affair stretching coast to coast, began in mid-September. Almost immediately things began to go wrong. On October 7, in Providence, Rhode Island, Harry and Bess had dinner with two writers of horror fiction, H. P. Lovecraft and C. M. Eddy, Jr., both of whom had previously done some ghostwriting for Harry and were now working for him on a book about superstition. After supper Bess fell ill from ptomaine poisoning, and Harry was up all night nursing her. Four days later he broke a bone in his ankle while preparing to do the Water Torture Cell act at the Capitol Theater in Albany. He carried on despite the fracture, limping from performance to performance, first in Albany and then in Schenectady, New York.

On Tuesday, October 19, his second day in Montreal, he gave a well-attended lecture at the McGill University student union. One of the students, Samuel Smilovitz, sketched him at the podium. Observing intently, Smilovitz noted the sickly appearance of the lecturer, who hobbled onto the stage and looked out over the audience with a "drawn face and dark shadows under tired eyes." Smilovitz recalled Houdini saying, "If I were to die tomorrow, the Spiritualists would declare an international holiday!" That night Harry made the last entry in his diary: "I spoke for an hour, my leg broken."

When Harry was shown Smilovitz's drawing, he invited the artist to visit him later in the week in his dressing room at the Princess Theatre—he wanted a portrait made for his collection. Smilovitz appeared at the theater on Friday morning, October 22, accompanied by a friend. Houdini was reclining on his dressing room couch, looking through his mail. While Smilovitz sketched, Houdini talked—about himself, his exploits. Another McGill student, J. Gordon Whitehead, knocked on the dressing room door; he had come to return a borrowed book. A talkative fellow, Whitehead was full of questions. He asked, "Is it true, Mr. Houdini, that you can resist the hardest blows struck to the abdomen?" Instead of denying that he possessed that particular talent, Houdini talked generally about his strength and offered to let the three students feel his famous forearms and back. But Whitehead persisted and asked, "Would you mind if I delivered a few blows to your abdomen, Mr. Houdini?" He accepted the challenge—just as he'd accepted the challenge posed by Rahman Bey and so many others before him—whereupon Whitehead leapt forward and pummeled him, punching him in the stomach until Houdini motioned for him to stop and told him, his voice barely audible, "That will do."

Smilovitz and his friend, shocked by Whitehead's behavior, stayed only until the sketch was completed. Houdini looked at it and said, "You made me look a little tired in this picture. The truth is, I don't feel so well." Nor did he feel well during Saturday night's performance. In both intermissions he slumped on the dressing room couch, sweat beading on his brow. After the show he was too unwell to dress himself unassisted. Yet he boarded the night train for Detroit. Because his stomachache worsened aboard the train, Bess sent a wire asking for a doctor to meet them in the morning.

The physician who examined Harry on the floor of his dressing room in the Garrick Theater that afternoon explained that acute appendicitis was most likely to blame for Harry's abdominal pain and 102-degree fever, but instead of seeking treatment at the hospital as recommended, Harry remained at the theater, telling the manager that he would go on with the show. Every ticket had been sold—he would not let his audience down. By the time the curtain rose on act 1 of HOUDINI, the star's temperature was 104. He completed the show but collapsed in the wings after each act. (The *Detroit News*, reviewing the night's performance, noted that the star was "a little hoarse and more than a little tired.") At the stage door, instead of taking the waiting ambulance, he hailed a taxi for the short ride to the Statler Hotel, where the house physician was so alarmed that he asked Dr. Charles Kennedy, chief of surgery at Grace Hospital, to come immediately to Houdini's suite. Kennedy arrived at three o'clock in the morning and told Houdini to go at once to the hospital, but Houdini insisted on telephoning his own doctor in New York for a second opinion.

Despite all this late-night urgency, it wasn't until three o'clock on the afternoon of Monday the 25th—eleven hours after he was admitted to the hospital—that he was operated on. By then it was far too late. He'd mistimed his escape. The appendix had burst, spilling bacterial pus into the abdominal cavity. Peritonitis had set in, which in the days before antibiotics was tantamount to a death sentence.

Uncomplaining and optimistic despite the pain and the grim prognosis, he lived for another six days, enduring a second operation to relieve "paralysis of the bowels." He died early in the afternoon of Sunday, October 31, 1926. He was fifty-two—a year younger than his father had been when he lost his job as rabbi of the Appleton congregation.

The cause of death was listed as "Diffuse peritonitis (Streptococcic)," which is correct. Legend, however, has assigned a different cause of death, attributing the appendicitis to the sucker punch landed by J. Gordon Whitehead. Even today it's not uncommon to read that Whitehead's punch ruptured Houdini's appendix.

Harry died from peritonitis because he was reluctant to see a doctor and, when he finally did, refused to follow the medical advice he was given. It's impossible to say when his appendix burst, but it could not have been on October 22, when Whitehead's punch landed—not even Houdini could survive nine days with a ruptured appendix. Perhaps it burst on the night train, somewhere between Montreal and Detroit, perhaps during his final performance, onstage at the Garrick Theater, perhaps afterward in the suite at the Statler. And the cause of the appendicitis? Anyone who contends that it was brought on by a powerful blow to the abdomen is buying into a very dubious medical diagnosis. The case for "traumatic appendicitis" is unproven: "No causal link has . . . been found between trauma and appendicitis," according to a surgeon's recent review of Houdini's case, "and the fact that these two events occurred within days of each other must be seen as coincidence." The sucker punch and the bacterial infection of the appendix may have occurred at approximately the same time, or the punch could have been delivered before the infection set in—but there's no medical evidence to suggest that the former caused the latter.

Bess, however, had a $25,000 reason to claim that Houdini's death was due to accident rather than illness: double indemnity. Harry's insurance policy (issued by New York Life) paid out $25,000 extra—twice the standard compensation—in case of "accidental demise." And so Bess, with the help of Harry's lawyer, Bernard Ernst, set out to establish that a blow to the abdomen killed him. New York Life eventually agreed to pay out the accident indemnity, a boon to the bereaved Bess and to conspiracy theorists everywhere.

Was J. Gordon Whitehead an agent of the Spiritualists? Many thought so. Others believed that the sucker punch was guided to its target by an angry spirit hovering in the dressing room of the Princess Theatre. Arthur Conan Doyle was convinced that the spirit world was "incensed" against Houdini, and that his death was "most certainly decreed from the other side." That it was Halloween the day Harry died was another coincidence destined to excite mumbo jumbo.

He was embalmed in Detroit and laid out in his $2,500 bronze burial casket, which happened to be in storage in a Detroit warehouse. In the casket he traveled by Pullman car to Grand Central Station, then on to a funeral parlor on the Upper West Side. On Thursday, November 4, he lay in state at the Elks Lodge no. 1 on West 43rd Street; as many as two thousand mourners filed past the open coffin. (All of this planned with utter disregard for Jewish law and custom.) The pallbearers, among them Adolph Zukor and Martin Beck, who'd given Harry his big break in vaudeville, carried the casket, piled high with flowers, out to the waiting hearse.

He was buried in the Machpelah Cemetery in Queens, alongside his beloved mother and his father, the grave marked by the grandiose granite exedra he'd designed, with its weeping female figure in marble, slumped beneath the marble bust of the Great Houdini.

10

Ever After

Houdini performed his last-ever suspended straitjacket escape on a bright sunny day in early April 1925, dangling from a scaffold projecting from the fourth floor of the *Indianapolis News* building on Washington Street in downtown Indianapolis. He'd added a new wrinkle: a $10 prize for the best photograph of the stunt. Three days later, from the stage of B. F. Keith's Theatre, he announced the winner.

Robert A. Twente's prizewinning photo shows a stampede of spectators jamming the street, filling the frame, a sea of heads, most with hats or caps on, necks craned to see a small trussed figure hanging overhead. The *News* estimated that the crowd numbered twelve thousand; that may be an exaggeration, like so much Houdini lore, but Twente's photo makes it look as if all of Indianapolis has turned out to see the living legend self-liberate.

The photo is a telling historical artifact—but it says very

little about Houdini. He's a tiny blurred figure, barely discern-
able, dangling in front of the third-floor windows of a sandstone
building just right of center. The shadow he casts, more vivid
than the man himself, makes it look as though he were arching
his back, his spasmodic thrashings already begun, but in fact
he's hanging straight up and down—the shadow is crooked only
because it falls on the cornice of the building.

The fact that Houdini is tiny and indistinct is perfectly
apt. It reminds us that his performances were ephemeral; all
that remains of his special genius is photos like this one, and a
few grainy, jerky moving pictures. He left behind no body of
work—unless you count the ghostwritten books and the films
he starred in, which were mediocre at best. Magic is ephemeral, and daredevil stunts like jailbreaks, bridge jumps, and suspended straitjacket escapes even more so. We can read about

them in contemporary accounts, but it's hard to get a sense of how thrilling they must have been to watch live. A winch turns, and with every turn a small man with his arms pinioned is hoisted higher, feet first. Dangling head down three stories above the sidewalk, he's in a deadly predicament that he himself has carefully planned and arranged. A pause, then wild jackknifing gyrations. Then the arms flung wide, like Christ on the cross upside down. The straitjacket drops, the sign that it's all over, that the manufactured danger has passed. The winch turns again, and the small man is lowered to the pavement while the crowd cheers.

An absurd artificial drama, and yet Twente's photo shows the citizens of Indianapolis apparently mesmerized, riveted by the prospect of witnessing imminent death averted. They may have been hoping for a grim conclusion, or for the catharsis of a narrow escape.

Houdini was not interested in the meaning of his stunts, and in a sense they were meaningless. They accomplished nothing. They advanced no cause, proved no point. And yet they drew enormous crowds in cities all over the country, crowds that formed hours before the event and dispersed slowly, with much head-scratching about the self-liberator's methods.

The lure of celebrity surely accounts for the size of the throng: they came to watch someone famous do something dangerous. Vaudeville had made Houdini famous; the movies spread his fame further. His name, now synonymous with escape, had passed into everyday language—he was on the tip of your tongue. And he mattered: he was making headlines in newspapers nationwide with his war against fraudulent mediums. Naturally, you would go to see him if you lived near Indianapolis and he was coming to town, promising to risk his life for your entertainment, for free. You had to be on hand in case this turned out to be a black day in history: the day Houdini died.

And what happens when the live performances come to an end, when the star is underground, sealed in a casket he can't escape?

* * *

The mythologizing began within a few years of his death, first in a biography based partly on Bess's recollections, partly on his diary and other documents. Harold Kellock's *Houdini, His Life-Story* (1928) is hagiographic and filled with exaggerations, half truths, and outright falsehoods, all flattering to the subject and his beloved, doting wife. Their marriage, according to this account, was bliss. Perhaps it was, though Harry's affair with Charmian London, his fulsome displays of devotion to Bess (all those florid declarations of undying love), Bess's quick temper, her professional retreat to the shadows, and her drinking—which got worse as Harry's fame grew—raise the suspicion that the relationship was neither as happy nor as simple as they claimed. Kellock reported that Bess found one last letter from Harry among his personal effects:

> Sweetheart, when you read this I shall be dead. Dear Heart, do not grieve; I shall be at rest by the side of my beloved parents, and wait for you always—remember! I loved only two women in my life: my mother and my wife. Yours, in Life, Death, and Ever After.

Marriage can be as mysterious as magic, but surely Bess grew weary of sharing her husband's love with his mother—and coming second, even after his death.

Kellock's book is the one Harry himself would have written (or rather hired a ghostwriter to write); it repeats his favorite false claims, including the fib that he was born in Appleton. This biography became the basis of the Technicolor Tony Curtis and Janet Leigh film from 1953, which is frankly fictional and further blurred the public's idea of what Harry Houdini was actually like, and how he died. Hollywood's Houdini is a daredevil driven by an obscure obsession with the occult. He drowns inside the Chinese Water Torture Cell, in full view of the audience (and the anguished Bess). Despite the grim ending, the overall effect of the film was to glamorize both Houdinis. Leigh's Bess is a curvy blonde, not notably petite; Curtis's Harry a more polished, more Americanized version of the original. These avatars refreshed and extended Houdini's fame, and helped spark a mid-century craze for magic.

The story has since been told and retold on film and in books, including a half dozen full-length biographies, several television series, and a steady stream of fan fiction, including most recently a novel called *Mrs. Houdini* (2016) that promises to "take you into the heart of one of history's greatest love stories."

Houdini lives on in legend now, indistinct like the dangling figure in Twente's photo. Though the name is recognized by young and old, it's just a name—he is no longer culturally relevant, except to magic buffs, collectors of Houdiniana, and aficionados of the glory days of vaudeville. At this distance, he's impervious to our opinion. His name will survive because it's part of the language, but he himself will grow more and more obscure.

Although he was not interested in the meaning of his stunts, others always have been. His self-liberation has most often been interpreted as a parable about breaking free—free from constraints either external (capitalism, bigotry) or internal (repression, self-doubt). The fact that Houdini stretched out his wrists for the handcuffs and walked willingly into the jail cell does nothing to diminish the power of the parable. Like Buster Keaton, like Charlie Chaplin, like Mickey Mouse, Harry Houdini was a beloved little guy defying authority, beating the odds, standing up to the bully, making it on his own. He triumphed over oppression, poverty, prejudice, slipping all those chains— but only figuratively. And without didactic intent. He never asked to be a poster boy for freedom, but he was enlisted all the same. Saul Bellow's Charlie Citrine, in an inspired meditation from *Humboldt's Gift,* wondered whether Houdini "hadn't had an intimation of the holocaust and was working out ways to escape from the death camps. Ah! If only European Jewry had learned what he knew."

Houdini wasn't trying to make a case or send a message or save Europe's Jews. He wasn't enacting a political or philosophical drama about liberation, let alone liberty. That kind of statement is spectacularly *absent* from the actual performance and from his own remarks. He liberated only himself.

The crusade against Spiritualists launched in the last five years of his life was in part motivated by a desire to do good: he hoped to help prevent the exploitation of the bereaved. During the Great War and after, he often raised money for charitable causes. He was at times suddenly and unexpectedly generous. But the long list of possible motives behind the escapes and death-defying stunts that made him world famous—a list that stretches from greed and vanity through narcissism and exhibitionism all the way to fear of failure and romantic yearning for transcendence—does not include a desire to improve the lot of his fellow man, or any other altruistic urge.

Undeterred by his campaign against them, Spiritualists have continued to argue that Houdini's stunts were, as Conan Doyle believed, a "demonstration of the occult"—proof of his supernatural powers and, by extension, evidence of the existence of a spirit world. Sixty years after his death, Houdini was still being dragooned into the ranks of spirit mediums. "Can a magician," asked Daniel Mark Epstein in a prizewinning 1986 essay, "by the ultimate perfection of a technique, generate a force that, at critical moments, will achieve a supernatural result?" For Epstein, as for many others, the meaning of Houdini's signature act lies in the possibility that his escapes might actually be miracles.

Some of the more plausible interpretations of his career

focus on his socioeconomic circumstances, some on his psycho-sexual makeup. Bette Howland, writing in *Commentary* in 2006, tied his significance to his milieu: "He was an expression—a phenomenon—of his times, the extreme that raises the particular to the level of the general. The very peculiarity of his act tells us that. And he was an American phenomenon." Howland argues that Houdini's life was "a spectacularly successful solution to the immigrant dilemma, the tragedy of the fathers, the liberty of the sons." She writes, "An escape is a success story," and suggests that his career was a microcosm of the explosion of immigrant energy in late nineteenth- and early twentieth-century America. This thesis does not, however, account for his international appeal. Houdini was a hugely popular export with a legion of fans in Britain, Germany, Russia, India, Japan—fans who were enthralled by his act but possibly not by his solution to the "immigrant dilemma."

More than forty years ago a Freudian analyst, Bernard C. Meyer, offered a top-to-toe "psychoanalytic portrait" of Harry. His book, *Houdini: A Mind in Chains* (1976), is furious in its denunciations of Harry's "limitless megalomania" and the ruthless patricide in *The Unmasking of Robert-Houdin*. It strips Houdini even of his good intentions with regard to Spiritualism: Dr. Meyer is convinced that his crusade was another symptom of a comprehensive psychopathology. (It was all about his mother.)

He treats Houdini as text, subjecting him to a rigorous close reading: "As a magician, and especially as an escapologist, his art invites an interpretation of its meaning, demanding the same attention to gesture and symbol that is accorded the dancer or the mime, [because] his performances, despite the patter that accompanied them, consisted essentially of a mute enactment of a few simple themes."

One of those simple themes was an endlessly reenacted rebirth, liberation from the womb. (Remember that Houdini's vaudeville act was nicknamed the "Death and Resurrection

Show.") The hidden meaning Dr. Meyer discovers in Houdini's performances tends to turn everything upside down or inside out. The self-liberator's escapes conceal a masochistic desire to be bound; his claustrophobia reveals itself as claustrophilia; and the repeated rebirths mask a desire to return to the womb. The overall effect of this analysis is to cram the outsized eccentricities of the wonderfully weird Houdini into a Freudian pigeonhole: he was suffering from an unresolved Oedipus complex. While it's true that his love for his mother was unusually, even scarily intense, and that he did his best to kill off a father figure, not everyone will find in the conjunction of those truths the key to his character or the wellspring of his tremendous appetite for success and the adoration of an audience.

And yet it's helpful to think, as Dr. Meyer does, of Houdini's "art" as a "counterphobic" strategy. It's possible that consciously or not Harry tried to master his anxieties by immersing himself in the very thing that terrified him. The dazzling tricks, the baffling escapes, the terrifying stunts—all these involved flirting with failure, which he was desperate to avoid. In some cases failure meant death, literally; in all cases failure was a figurative death, a public humiliation he could not endure.

* * *

Perhaps the most useful verdicts are the simplest, verdicts that take Houdini at face value, as a spellbinding performer who carved out for himself a niche in show business history by escaping from every conceivable constraint. Will Rogers, himself a colossally famous entertainer, called him "the greatest showman of our time by far." And indeed, Harry's most urgent desire, at home and in public, was to devise an enthralling spectacle. He thrived on attention. In his vaudeville days, if his act wasn't top billing, or if the crowds were thin, he wondered, "Is this . . . the first step toward oblivion?" He once wrote, "I have tried through many a sleepless night to invent schemes to make an audience appreciate some worthy effort of mine"—a bland, opaque remark that reveals nothing except the extent of his restless striving, the persistent itch that made him lie awake at night. Perhaps, as Adam Phillips has suggested, "the only thing one could do with Houdini was to be amazed by him."

Arthur Conan Doyle wrote at length about Houdini after his death, making a concerted effort to be evenhanded in his judgment, to see Harry clearly, to make sense of their short-lived friendship. Although he had become, briefly, Houdini's enemy, he never behaved badly, never abandoned his cherished principles of decency and fair play. Undeniably credulous, he was no fool. In *The Edge of the Unknown* (1930), he praised Houdini's "cheery urbanity" as well as his courage and generosity, calling him "one of the most remarkable men of whom we have any record." But he did not shrink from pointing out flaws:

> A prevailing feature of his character was a vanity which was so obvious and childish that it became more amusing than offensive. I can remember, for example, that when he introduced his brother to me, he did it by saying, "This is the brother of the great Houdini." This without any twinkle of humour and in a perfectly natural manner.
>
> This enormous vanity was combined with a passion for publicity which knew no bounds, and which must at all costs be gratified.

Conan Doyle's verdict, in the end, was mixed:

> Let me say . . . that in a long life which has touched every side of humanity, Houdini is far and away the most curious and intriguing character whom I have ever encountered. I have met better men, and I have certainly met very many worse ones, but I have never met a man who had such strange contrasts in his nature, and whose actions and motives it was more difficult to foresee or to reconcile.

He made no attempt to unravel this tangle of motives or to whitewash these contrasts. Already flummoxed by Harry while their friendship endured, Conan Doyle had written to him saying, "You are to me a perpetual mystery. No doubt you are to everyone." Harry's widow agreed. In a letter to Conan Doyle, trying once again to explain that it was not "psychic help" that had allowed her husband to perform his escapes, Bess wrote what may be taken as the last word on the subject: "It was Houdini himself that was the secret."

A NOTE ON SOURCES

HOUDINI, HIS LIFE-STORY (1928), the first Houdini biography, written by Harold Kellock in close collaboration with Bess and based in part on Houdini's journals and on his scrapbooks stuffed with news clippings, is charming, indispensable, and unreliable. No subsequent biographer can resist it, and none can trust it: many of the flattering stories it tells have since been debunked.

Thirty years later, William Lindsay Gresham, author of the noir classic *Nightmare Alley*, published *Houdini, the Man Who Walked through Walls* (1959), a thoroughly enjoyable novelistic account, tilted toward Harry's life in show business, with special emphasis on the seedy early years. (Gresham was obsessed with carnival and sideshow freaks.) The next biographer, Milbourne Christopher, was himself a magician and a historian of magic; like Harry, he served as president of SAM. His *Houdini: The Untold Story* (1969) is detailed and persuasive, though now somewhat dated. Bernard C. Meyer, MD, put Harry on the couch for his perceptive and unforgiving "psychoanalytic portrait," *Houdini: A*

Mind in Chains (1976). *Death and the Magician: The Mystery of Houdini* (1981), by Raymund Fitzsimons, is brief and breezy despite its emphasis on Houdini's "fascination" with death. Either Fitzsimons was unaware of Dr. Meyer's contribution or he ignored it in favor of his own, less orthodox brand of pathography.

Ruth Brandon published *The Life and Many Deaths of Harry Houdini* in 1993. A passionate and personal book, interspersed with autobiographical vignettes, it elegantly selects from previous biographies and adds new material gleaned from Houdini's correspondence as well. Brandon argues unconvincingly that Harry was impotent. Kenneth Silverman's authoritative and exhaustive *Houdini!!! The Career of Ehrich Weiss* (1996) is a sympathetic yet unflinching biography that replaced legend, anecdote, and the haze of myth with carefully researched and verified fact. It was Silverman, for example, who discovered Harry's affair with Charmian London (thereby scuppering Brandon's theory about impotence). If the book has a flaw, it's the urge to document every Houdini performance and describe every trick (without giving away any secrets, a taboo for Silverman, who was an amateur magician in his youth).

The Secret Life of Houdini: The Making of America's First Superhero (2006), by William Kalush and Larry Sloman, although otherwise meticulously researched, takes as its premise the bizarre, unfounded notion that Harry was a spy in the employ of the Secret Service, and also that he was the victim of a cabal of Spiritualists who plotted his untimely death. The book is punctuated by imaginative reconstructions of events, elaborate dramatizations that veer uncomfortably close to fiction.

In addition to those eight biographies, I've relied on a number of books that either feature Harry prominently or focus on a particular aspect of his career. Jim Steinmeyer's highly intelligent and entertaining *Hiding the Elephant: How Magicians Invented the Impossible and Learned to Disappear* (2003) offers a capsule biography of Harry as well as trenchant observations on his magic. ("Watching him play the part of an elegant conjuror was a bit like watching a wrestler play the violin.") Adam Phillips's provocative *Houdini's*

Box: The Art of Escape (2001) juxtaposes challenging ideas about Harry with case studies from Phillips's practice as a psychotherapist. John F. Kasson's *Houdini, Tarzan, and the Perfect Man: The White Male Body and the Challenge of Modernity in America* (2001) is a first-rate cultural history that examines a crucial aspect of Houdini's performance: his nakedness. The story of Harry's vexed friendship with Arthur Conan Doyle has been told many times; Conan Doyle himself did the honors in *The Edge of the Unknown* (1930). The most recent account is Christopher Sandford's comprehensive *Houdini and Conan Doyle* (2011). The magician Bob Loomis devoted an entire three-hundred-page book, *Houdini's Final Incredible Secret* (2016), to the elaborate trick Harry performed for Conan Doyle in the library of his Harlem brownstone. Anyone wanting to know everything there is to know about the medium Margery and her epic battle with Harry should consult David Jaher's artful and meticulous *The Witch of Lime Street: Séance, Seduction, and Houdini in the Spirit World* (2015). Bruce MacNab's *The Metamorphosis: The Apprenticeship of Harry Houdini* (2012) is a careful and considered account of the ill-fated twelve-week tour Harry and Bess made of the Maritime Provinces in 1896. Derek Tait doggedly tracked Harry's travels in the United Kingdom in *The Great Houdini: His British Tours* (2017); Leann Richards did something similar in *Houdini's Tour of Australia* (2018). Ann Beedham revealed the part played by a British teenager in the development of the suspended straitjacket escape in *Randini: The Man Who Helped Houdini* (2009).

Sadly, I missed *Houdini: Art and Magic*, a 2010 exhibition at the Jewish Museum in New York, but the show's handsome catalogue, *Houdini*, contains valuable historical essays by Kenneth Silverman and Alan Brinkley, as well as many extraordinary photographs of Harry onstage and off. Other important essays include Daniel Mark Epstein's "The Case of Harry Houdini" in the *New Criterion* (1986); Bette Howland's "The Escape Artist" in *Commentary* (2006); and Robert Gottlieb's "The Secrets of Houdini" in the *New York Review of Books* (2011).

Anyone who writes anything about Houdini must inevitably

consult the website created and curated by John Cox, *Wild about Harry* (www.wildabouthoudini.com), a tremendous, continually expanding trove of material about Houdini and his world. No factoid is too minute for Cox, no spinoff too obscure; a devourer of all things Houdini, he is hugely generous with his treasure. Also on the web, and also invaluable: the digital archive of the *New York Times* (https://timesmachine.nytimes.com/browser), where Harry pops up with astonishing frequency, his prodigious talent as a self-promoter still reaping rewards nearly a century later.

ILLUSTRATIONS

page 79: The Water Torture Cell. (Library of Congress)

page 82: Houdini jumping from Harvard Bridge into the Charles River, April 1908. (Courtesy of the History Museum at the Castle)

page 87: Flying the Voisin biplane in Australia, March 1910. (Library of Congress)

page 97: Theodore, aka Dash, aka Hardeen, with Bess in front of the Houdini/Weiss monument, Machpelah Cemetery. (Library of Congress)

page 102: Houdini preparing for his "Daring Dive" in a packing crate, July 1914. (Library of Congress)

page 104: Suspended straitjacket escape. (Courtesy of the History Museum at the Castle)

page 106: Houdini and Jennie the vanishing elephant. (New York Public Library)

page 116: Houdini in *The Master Mystery*. (Library of Congress)

page 120: *The Man from Beyond* film poster. (Harry Ransom Center, the University of Texas at Austin)

page 123: The world-famous movie star Harry Houdini. (National Portrait Gallery, Smithsonian Institution)

page 128: Charmian London. (Courtesy of the Sonoma County Library)

page 133: Arthur Conan Doyle and Houdini. (Harry Ransom Center, the University of Texas at Austin)

page 142: Conan Doyle and Houdini in Atlantic City, June 1922. (www.wildabouthoudini.com)

page 164: Houdini and Margery, July 1924. (www.wildabouthoudini.com)

page 170: "One of the most accomplished magicians in the world." (New York Public Library)

page 185: Suspended straitjacket escape, Indianapolis, April 1925. (Courtesy of the *Indianapolis Star*)

ACKNOWLEDGMENTS

GEORGES BORCHARDT, a most excellent agent, conspired with Ileene Smith, editor and impresario of the Jewish Lives series, to hook me up with the prodigious Harry Houdini—I'm enduringly grateful to both of them, and to Leon Black, munificent patron of the series.

Heather Gold was my patient guide to the wonders and mysteries of Yale University Press. This book took shape thanks to her and her friendly and supercompetent colleagues: copyeditor Robin DuBlanc; production manager Katie Golden; proofreader Erica Hanson; indexer Kara Pekar; publicist Elizabeth Pelton; production editor Jeffrey Schier; and text and jacket designer Mary Valencia.

While I was writing and later, while I was gathering illustrations, friends and strangers helped me out in various ways. Here are their names: Erin Beasley, Jane Berridge, Eric Colleary, John Cox, Peter Filkins, Elizabeth Garver, Mary Haegert, Susan Halpert, Nadia Kousari, Simone Kremkau, Wendy Lesser, Dustin Mack,

Aubrey Martinson, Cristina Meisner, Dawn Mitchell, Samantha Shea, and Alexis Valentine.

Tim Duggan graciously allowed me to interrupt another project to tackle this one.

Robert Gottlieb and Chloë Ashby are both excellent readers. They were kind enough to cast an eye over the manuscript and offer advice and encouragement. Before I even got started, Bob helpfully pointed out that everything I needed to know about Houdini could be found in his *New York Review of Books* essay; he was right, as always.

My father, Louis Begley, and my stepmother, Anka Muhlstein, also read the manuscript, and generously provided shelter and sustenance as well as the benefit of their collective wisdom.

Anne Cotton is at the beginning and end of everything I write, and this is no exception.

INDEX

Page numbers in *italics* followed by *f* indicate photographs.

JEWISH LIVES is a prizewinning series of interpretative biography designed to explore the many facets of Jewish identity. Individual volumes illuminate the imprint of Jewish figures upon literature, religion, philosophy, politics, cultural and economic life, and the arts and sciences. Subjects are paired with authors to elicit lively, deeply informed books that explore the range and depth of the Jewish experience from antiquity to the present.

Jewish Lives is a partnership of Yale University Press and the Leon D. Black Foundation. Ileene Smith is editorial director. Anita Shapira and Steven J. Zipperstein are series editors.